CW00926549

Shetland
Lace

Photography by John Coutts

The Shetland Times Ltd
Lerwick
1996

First published 1993
Reprinted 1996



All photography by John Coutts

Cover design by the Stafford Partnership

ISBN 0 900662 89 1



British Library Cataloguing-in-Publication Data
A catalogue record for this book is available from the British Library

Printed and published by
The Shetland Times Ltd., Prince Alfred Street, Lerwick, Shetland ZE1 0EP.

# CONTENTS

# DEDICATION

Dedicated to the memory of a very dear friend and a much-loved lady, Nellie Tulloch, late of Aywick and Burravoe, Yell, who introduced me to cobweb lace knitting and encouraged me to continue working in this medium.

Unfortunately, Nellie is no longer with us, but I like to think that she would have approved of the contents of this volume.

# FOREWORD

Once in a while, someone produces a book or a collection of patterns which grab your attention and hold a special place in your heart. This is one such book. These designs have their roots firmly planted in tradition, yet each one can hold its own valued place in today's modern family life.

If you can follow a basic knitting pattern, you can do Shetland Lace.

The patterns in this book have been designed with care and consideration for the knitter, with close attention to detail. They are written logically and clearly, and best of all, instructions are given row by row. So, when the time comes to put down your knitting, it is very easy to pick it up again later without losing your place.

The abbreviations are given in their regional version and may look unfamiliar to some people. But don't be put off — it's just an alternative way of describing familiar stitches. It doesn't take long to get used to them.

The appeal of Shetland Lace is obvious, yet its delicacy belies its strength. It allows the knitter to create something beautifully special which is light and warm to wear, yet can be washed time and time again without coming to any harm, and still maintain its "family-heirloom" status. You will have made something which is more than just a piece of knitting, it will be an art form, a garment which has been worked in the same way by generations before you, and your participation helps to keep this historic craft alive.

I made my first attempt at knitting a 1-ply cobweb lace shawl several years ago and was thrilled at my success. The knitting needles weren't as fine as I expected them to be and, once I'd grown used to the fineness of the wool, I was hooked. At first I didn't think the finished shawl was much to look at, and it wasn't until it was washed and dressed that its true beauty was revealed. The sense of achievement was immense — and, best of all, it is within the capabilities of most knitters.

It's easy to become passionate about Shetland Lace and if this book doesn't tempt you to have a go, then nothing will. I'm sure that those knitters who already knit lace will be delighted with this well-balanced collection. The question is . . . which one do you make first?

*Bea Neilson*
*Knitting Editor, "The People's Friend"*
*June, 1993*

# INTRODUCTION

This book is intended to be a "Book of Patterns" featuring specially-designed garments. I make no apologies for not covering the "History of Shetland Lace" — many others have researched it well and produced volumes on the subject.

It is hoped that interested knitters will find something they would like to make from this selection.

All the patterns in this book have been designed especially for use with either Shetland 1-ply cobweb lace wool or Shetland 2-ply lace wool. Both the cobweb and 2-ply lace are available from the suppliers — Messrs. Jamieson & Smith (Shetland Wool Brokers) Ltd, 90 North Road, Lerwick, Shetland (Telephone Lerwick (0595) 3579).

The 100 per cent pure new wool is from sheep born and raised in the Shetland Isles. The raw wool is sent by the Shetland Wool Brokers to Hunter's of Brora who are commissioned to spin specially for them, into the various weights and required colours.

All pattern rows are detailed — this may seem tedious to the experienced knitter, but hopefully it is more useful for those new to this kind of knitting.

Please read instructions carefully before starting to work on a garment. Notes are provided to help you.

Enjoy your knitting!!

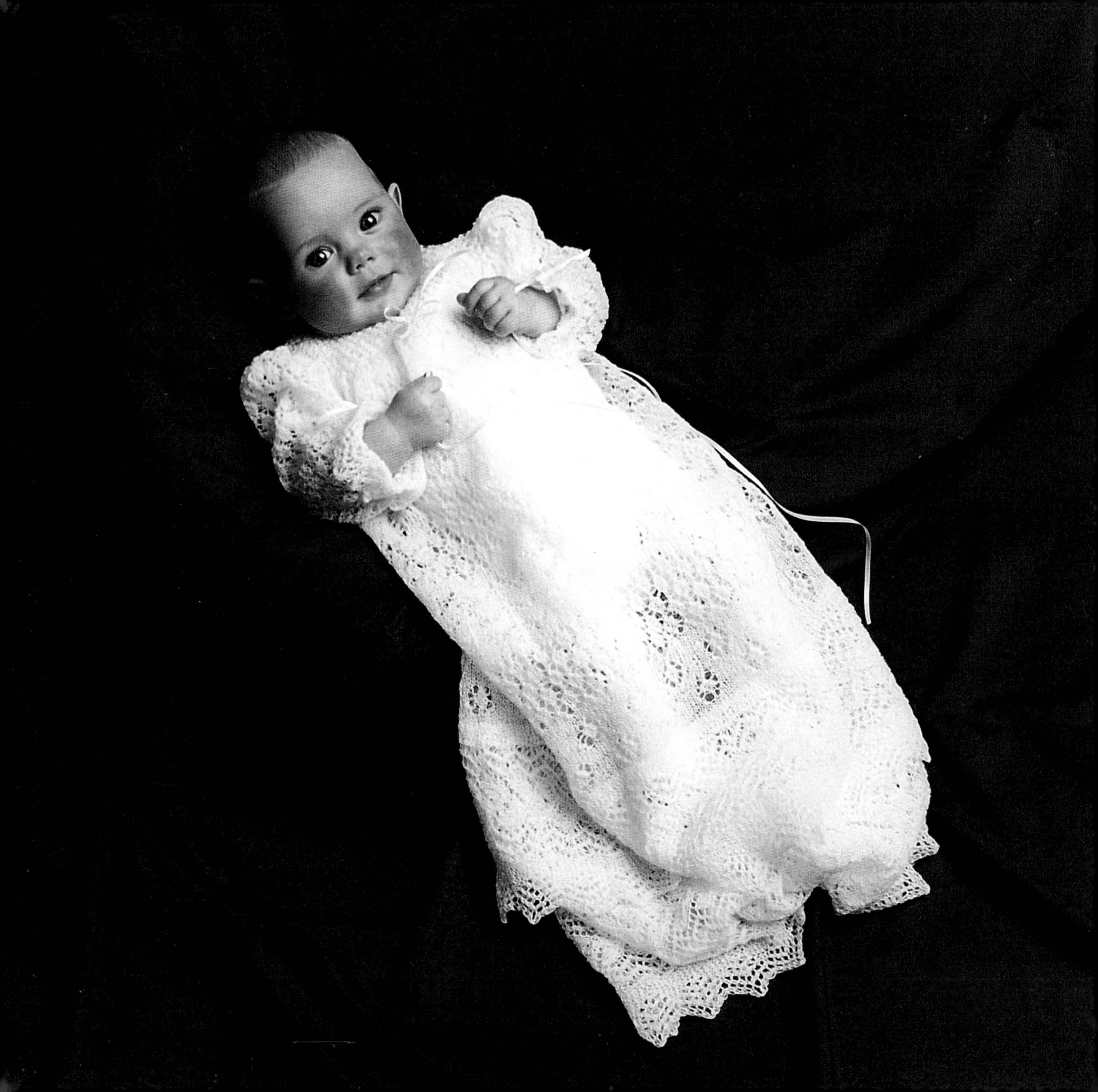

## ABOUT THE DESIGNS

### *The Sheelagh Shawl* — Page 3

This shawl is knitted in 1-ply cobweb wool and is designed as a lady's evening shawl as well as being suitable for a baby's christening.

In days gone by it was not uncommon for a similar garment to be used for a bride's wedding veil and then kept for the christening of the couple's babies. It would often be kept as an heirloom and handed down to the next generation in due course.

### *The Sheelagh Robe* — Page 13

This christening robe is designed to match the Sheelagh shawl.

The above two garments can be produced as an heirloom set to be kept in the family for future generations.

### *Fine Lace Stole or Scarf* — Page 27

These garments are designed to give the traditional look although simplified by the fact that they are knitted continuously without any grafted joins.

The pattern for each garment is detailed. In addition, an alternative stitch pattern is offered for the centre panel of the scarf.

### *Fine Lace Scarf* — Page 33

The detailed pattern is given for the smaller version of the stole on page 27. At the end of the pattern there is a detail of a stitch pattern for the centre of the scarf offering the knitter an alternative without alteration to the remainder of the original.

### *The Brora Black Shawl* — Page 41

This shawl was designed specially for use with the first black 1-ply cobweb lace wool spun by Hunter's of Brora for Messrs. Jamieson & Smith of Lerwick.

It is suitable for ladies' evening wear, and can also be knitted in the pale green shade of cobweb, or worked in white for use as a baby's christening shawl.

### *The Gibbie Shawl* — Page 51

The author was requested to produce a cobweb lace shawl pattern by a gentleman well-known to many Shetland knitters, and it was decided that the pattern should be given his name.

The shawl is suitable for a baby's christening or for use as a shoulder shawl for an adult.

### *Baby's Lace Jacket & Bonnet* — Page 59

A cobweb lace outfit for that special occasion — the christening. The jacket is worked in one piece up to the underarms and the remainder is fully detailed. Although it is not the same design as the Sheelagh robe, it could be used with it or with any other christening outfit.

## *Cobweb Lace Wrap*

Page 71

This wrap is triangular in shape and affords the wearer the choice of using it as a shoulder wrap or, as it weighs only 3½ ounces it is ideal to wear over head and shoulders without fear of destroying a hair style! At the same time it does give a comforting warmth.

## *The Philip & Michael Shawl*

Page 85

This 2-ply lace baby shawl is made in the more traditional style of border lace, main border and square centre panel.

It was originally designed for the author's two grandsons with the variation of stitch in the centre panel to personalise each one.

## *Circular Shaded Shawl*

Page 91

Old Shale stitch is used in the design of the circular shaded shawl. The stitch pattern is adjusted to achieve the perfect circular shape.

## *The Belinda Skirt*

Page 97

The circular shaded system has been further evolved to produce the Belinda skirt.

## *The Belinda Cape*

Page 101

A further progression of the circular theme produces the cape which combines with the skirt to make an outfit suitable for a wedding or for evening wear.

## *Belinda Shoulder Shawl*

Page 107

This triangular shoulder shawl offers an alternative easy-to-wear garment to use with the Belinda skirt.

The shoulder shawl uses the same Old Shale stitch pattern but the design produces a completely different effect.

It can also be knitted in 1-ply cobweb lace wool and will weight only 1½ ounces.

## *Cockleshell Stole*

Page 117

This particular stole has been designed to vary the usual system of working the "shells" across the width of the garment, repeated until the desired length is reached, or worked from both ends and joined in the centre.

Working the pattern repeats as detailed gives a fine scalloped edge to the length of the stole and does not involve any seam grafting.

*The Brora Black, the Gibbie shawl, the stole and scarf set and the Pam (now known as the Philip and Michael shawl) were first produced for Jamieson and Smith, and are included with their permission.*

# STITCH PATTERNS

The following stitch patterns are detailed for the benefit of those not familiar with them. The various stitches given are those used in the preceding patterns and will afford an apportunity for the knitter to work the patterns before starting on the garments.

It must be noted that these samples are shown as they would be worked "in the straight". Most of the designs in this book are for working "in the round", and therefore where "purl" rows are quoted in the sample these will become "knit" rows in the garment patterns.

The number of stitches required to work the patterns is given – no "spacer" stitches are included, but generally an odd number is recommended. Example: roundel stitch requires 7 stitches for one motif. If a "spacer" of 5 or 7 stitches is used, this allows a second sequence of motifs to be worked in a "staggered" position. Likewise, cat's paw can be worked in the "staggered" position to give a very simple, but effective, all-over result. (See stole – alternative centre panel.)

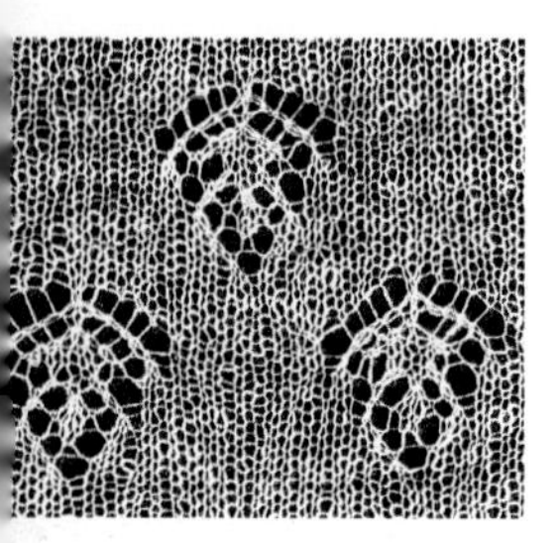

## SHETLAND FERN

No. of stitches required — 15 No. of rows — 16

Row 1 — Knit 7 c skp k6

Rows 2, 4, 6, 8 and 10 — Purl

Row 3 — Knit 5, T c k1 c TB k5

Row 5 — Knit 4, T c k3 c TB k4

Row 7 — Knit 4, c TB c s2kp c T c k4

Row 9 — Knit 2, T c k1 c TB, k1, T c k1 c TB k2

Row 11 — Knit 2, c TB c TB, k3, T c T c k2

Row 12 — Purl 3, c PT c PT, purl 1, PTB c PTB c purl 3

Row 13 — Knit 4, c TB c s2kp c T c k4

Row 14 — Purl 5, c PT, purl 1, PTB c purl 5

Row 15 — Knit 6, c s2kp c, knit 6

Row 16 — Purl

When this pattern is worked "in the round" (as for Sheelagh shawl and robe — page 3 & 13) the purl stitches of even-numbered rows are worked as knit rows.

If working repeats of the Fern stitch, spacer stitches between sequences are recommended to accentuate the individual ferns.

Shetland Fern stitch can be used in many ways — in panels to form attractive ends for stoles or scarves; as individual inset patterns in baby garments or adult jumpers or tops. It can be set in various motif shapes to form an interesting feature of garments knitted in all-over lace patterns.

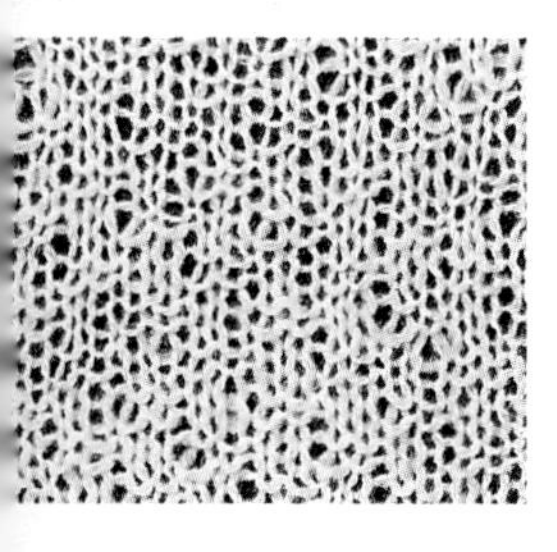

## BASKET STITCH

No. of stitches required — multiple of 8 No. of rows — 8

Rows 1, 2, 3 and 4 — (k4, p4), repeat ( ) as required

Rows 5, 6, 7 and 8 — (p4, k4), repeat ( ) as required

## DOUBLE MOSS STITCH

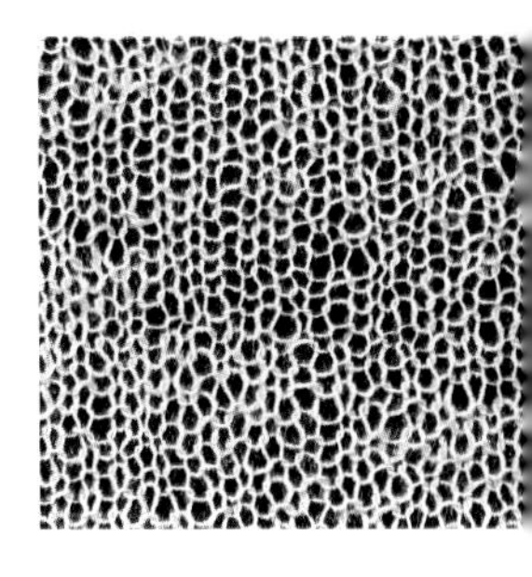

No. of stitches required — 4

No. of rows — 4

Rows 1 and 2 — (k2, p2), repeat ( ) as required

Rows 3 and 4 — (p2, k2), repeat ( ) as required

The above two stitch patterns, although not lacy ones, form very good centres to shawls and can be used for any garment requiring a firm edge or a contrast to the lacy portion of the design.

## SINGLE MOSS STITCH

No. of stitches required — any odd number

No. of rows — 2

Row 1 — (k1, p1), repeat to last st., k1

Row 2 — (k1, p1), repeat to last st., k1

Alternative for any even number of stitches —

Row 1 — (k1, p1), repeat to end

Row 2 — (p1, k1), repeat to end

Moss stitch offers a firm fabric for edging where ordinary ribbing is inappropriate.

## MINIATURE LEAF STITCH

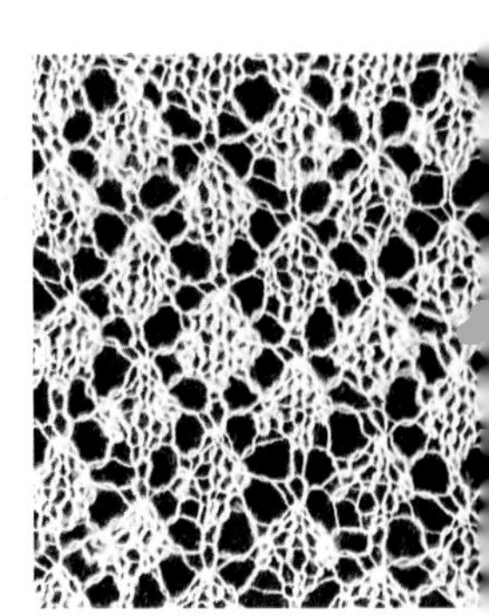

No. of stitches required — multiple of 6 + 1

No. of rows — 8

Row 1 — (k1 T c k1 c TB), repeat ( ) to last st., k1

Row 2 and every alternate row — Purl

Row 3 — Tc (k3 c s2kp c), repeat ( ) to last 5 sts., k3 c T

Row 5 — K1 (c TB k1 T c k1), repeat ( )

Row 7 — K2 (c s2kp c k3), repeat ( ) to last 5 sts., c s2kp c k2

Row 8 — Purl

This stitch is very useful as a break between other stitch patterns and is also very effective for sleeves of baby's garments.

**SPECIAL NOTE**: If working "in the round" refer to Miniature Leaf sequence of the Sheelagh robe (page 13) and note that all purl rows are knitted. The details above are for working "on the straight".

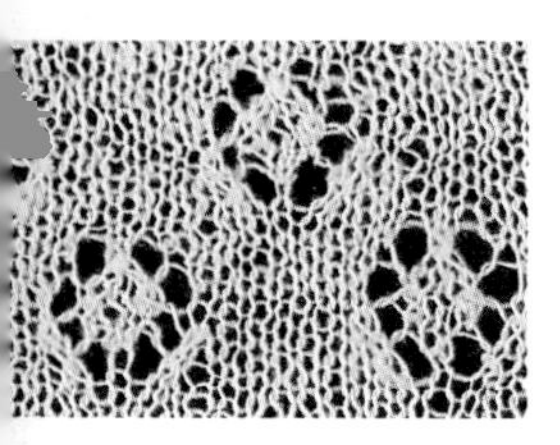

**ROUNDEL STITCH**

No. of stitches required — 12 No. of rows — 8

Row 1 — K4 T c k1 c TB k3

Row 2 and every alternate row — purl

Row 3 — K3 T c k3 c TB k2

Row 5 — K4 c TB k1 T c k3

Row 7 — K5 c s2kp c k4

Row 8 — Purl

The Roundel stitch, which is similar to Cat's Paw, is also a variation of Miniature Leaf stitch, being worked as individual motifs rather than a repeated all-over pattern.

It can be used in many ways — to form a panel (as in the wrap — page 71) or to give an attractive band of motifs (as in the Sheelagh shawl and robe (page 3 & 13)

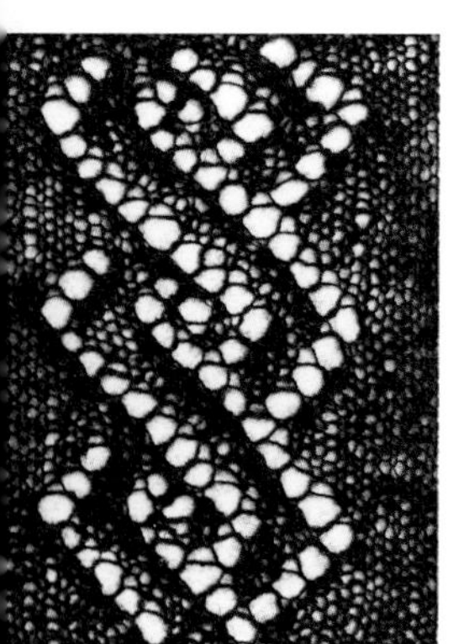

**DIAMOND CHAIN**

No. of stitches required — 18 No. of rows — 16

Row 1 — K6 c TB k2 c TB k6

Row 2 and every alternate row — Purl

Row 3 — K4 T c k1 c TB k2 c TB k5

Row 5 — K3 T c k3 c TB k2 c TB k4

Row 7 — K2 T c k2 T c k1, c TB k2 c TB k3

Row 9 — K1 T c k2 T c k3, c TB k2 c TB k2

Row 11 — K3 c TB k2 c TB c T c k2 T c T k1

Row 13 — K4 c TB k2 c s2kp c k2 T c k3

Row 15 — K5 c TB k2 c TB k1 T c k4

Row 16 — Purl

If this pattern is to be worked in more than one panel, it is advisable to work spacer stitches between the 18-stitch repeats.

This stitch makes a very attractive centre panel for a stole or scarf, but can also be used to vary end panels.

**PRINT OF THE WAVE**

No. of stitches required — multiple of 14 + 13 No. of rows — 12

Row 1 — K3 Tc Tc Tc (k1 T k3 T k1, c k1 c, Tc Tc) k4

Row 2 and every alternate row — purl.

Row 3 — K3 Tc Tc Tc (k1 T k1 T k1, c k3 c, Tc Tc) k4

Row 5 — K3 Tc Tc Tc (k1 s2kp k1, c k5 c, Tc Tc) k4

Row 7 — K4 cT cT (c k1 c, k1 T k3 T k1, cT cT) cT k3

Row 9 — K4 cT cT (c k3 c, k1 T k1 T k1, cT cT) cT k3

Row 11 — K4 cT cT (c k5 c, k1 s2kp k1, cT cT) cT k3

Row 12 — Purl

The above instructions are for one sequence of Print of the Wave; if working additional sequences the bracketed part ONLY is repeated, stitches before and after the brackets being worked at the start and end of the row as appropriate.

This stitch is very suitable for the centre panel of a stole or scarf, or incorporated into a border lace.

**RING STITCH**

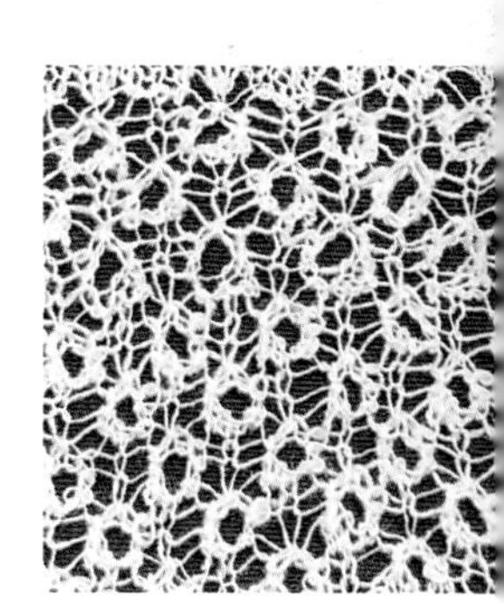

No. of stitches required — multiple of 6 + 1 No. of rows — 8

Row 1 — (k1 c T c 3T c), repeat ( ) k1

Row 2 — K1 (c T k1 T c k1), repeat ( )

Row 3 — K2 c 3T (c k3 c 3T), repeat ( ) c k2

Row 4 — K1 (T c k1 c T k1), repeat ( )

Row 5 — K1 T (c k1 c T c 3T), repeat ( ) c k1 c T k1

Row 6 — K1 (T c k1 c T k1), repeat ( )

Row 7 — T c k3 c (3T c k3 c), repeat ( ) T

Row 8 — K1 (c T k1 T c k1), repeat ( )

This is a very simple stitch and produces a very effective all-over pattern, suitable for scarves, stoles or other items. As detailed above it is NOT worked "in the round"

**NOTE**: A slightly slack tension is recommended.

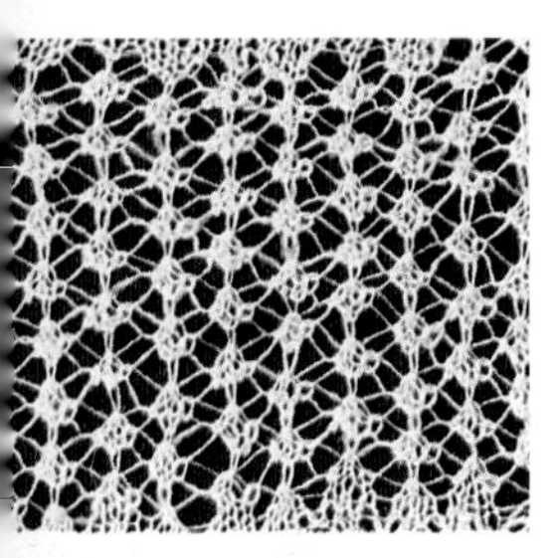

## BEAD STITCH

No. of stitches required — multiple of 6 + 1 | No. of rows — 4

Row 1 — K2 (c s2kp c k3), repeat ( ) to last 5 sts., c s2kp c k2

Row 2 — K1 (T c k1 c T k1), repeat ( )

Row 3 — T (c k3 c s2kp), repeat ( ) to last 6 sts., c k3 c T

Row 4 — K1 (c T k1 T c k1), repeat ( )

This is a very attractive all-over lace stitch and very simple to knit. It can also be used in panels or motifs (see Diamond Bead stitch below).

**NOTE**: The above instructions are for working "on the straight".

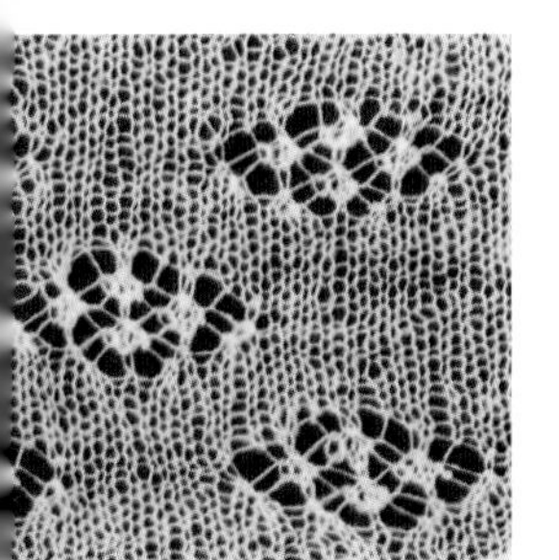

## DIAMOND BEAD STITCH

No. of stitches required — 15 | No. of rows — 8

The following sequence forms one motif of Diamond Bead. It is necessary to work at least two rows of stocking-stitch before and after the sequence, and it is recommended that if more than one sequence is to be worked spacers be used to separate them.

Row 1 — K5 T c k1 c T k5

Row 2 — P4 T c k3 c T P4

Row 3 — K2 T c k1 c T, k1, T c k1 c T k2

Row 4 — P1 T c k3 c s2kp c k3 c T p1

Row 5 — K2 c T k1 T c, k1, c T k1 T c k2

Row 6 — P3 c s2kp c k3, c s2kp c, p3

Row 7 — K5 c T k1 T c k5

Row 8 — P6 c s2kp c p6

This is a variation of Bead stitch — it forms an interesting motif, useful as a feature set into a stocking-stitch background.

## HORSESHOE STITCH

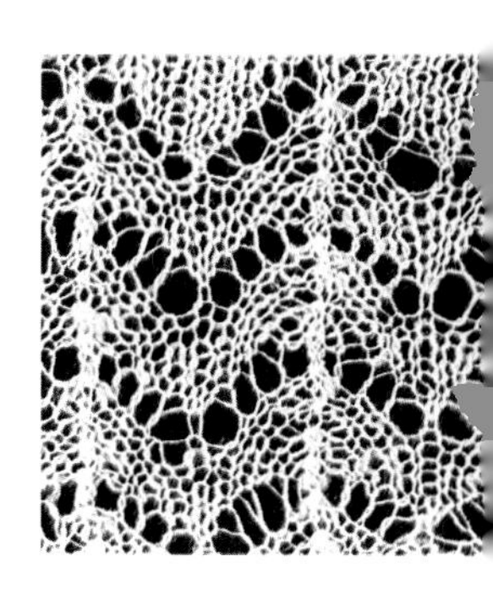

No. of stitches required — multiples of 10 + 1 No. of rows — 8

Row 1 — K1 (c k3 s2kp k3 c k1), repeat ( )

Row 2 and every alternate row — Purl

Row 3 — K1 (k1 c k2 s2kp k2 c k2), repeat ( )

Row 5 — K1 (k2 c k1 s2kp k1 c k3), repeat ( )

Row 7 — K1 (k3 c s2kp c k4), repeat ( )

Row 8 — Purl

**NOTE:** If working in the round "k1" at the beginning of rows 1, 3, 5 & 7 is omitted. The bracketed 10-stitch sequence may be repeated as many times as required.

This is a very easy stitch to work and can be used for almost any kind of lacy garment. One complete 8-row sequence forms a very pleasing scalloped border. Several repeats worked continuously in the 8-row sequence form a very good centre panel for a stole or scarf.

## BIRD'S EYE

No. of stitches required — multiple of 4 No. of rows — 4

**NOTE:** In the following 4-row sequence the number of stitches will fluctuate —

Rows 1 and 3 will reduce the number of stitches

Rows 2 and 4 will increase the count back to normal

Row 1 — (T c T), repeat ( ) as required

Row 2 — (k1, k1 and p1 into made stitch, k1), repeat ( )

Row 3 — K2 (T c T), repeat ( ) to last 2 sts., k2

Row 4 — K2 (k1, k1 and p1 into made stitch, k1), repeat ( ) to last 2 sts., k2

This is a very useful stitch where a degree of stretch is an advantage — i.e. the yoke of a baby garment or the bodice of a baby's jacket — it keeps its shape well, but at the same time it allows a certain amount of give — an aid to dressing an infant! It can also be used as a filler stitch in conjunction with other patterns.

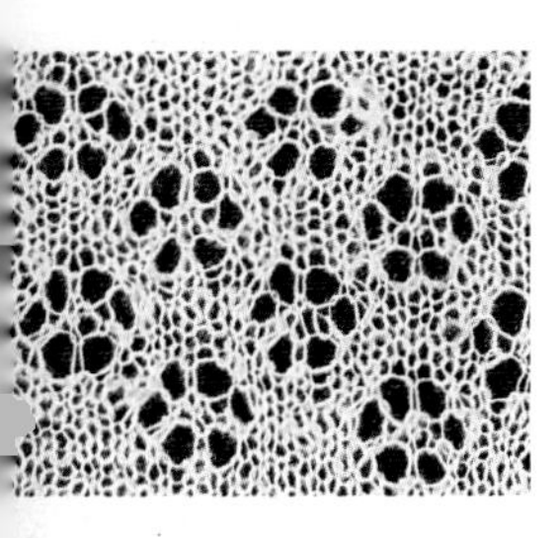

**CAT'S PAW**

No. of stitches required — multiple of 10 + 7 No. of rows — 6

Row 1 — K1 (k5 T c k1 c T), repeat ( ) to last 6 sts., k6

Rows 2, 4 and 6 — purl

Row 3 — K2 (k3 T c k3 c T), repeat ( ) to last 5 sts., k5

Row 5 — K1 (k5 T c k1 c T), repeat ( ) to last 6 sts., k6

**NOTE**: To work as an all-over staggered pattern, it is necessary to work rows 7-12 (below) AFTER rows 1-6 above.

No. of stitches required — multiple of 10 + 7 No. of rows — 12
Work rows 1-6, then follow with:

Row 7 — K1 (T c k1 c T k5), repeat ( ) to last 6 sts., T c k1 c T, k1

Rows 8, 10 and 12 — purl

Row 9 — (T c k3 c T k3), repeat ( ) to last 7 sts., T c k3 c T

Row 11 — K1 (T c k1 c T k5), repeat ( ) to last 6 sts., T c k1 c T, k1

This simple 6-row (or 12-row) pattern is a very old Shetland stitch. It can be used as an individual motif or incorporated in an all-over pattern. Used in blocks of various shapes it can produce many varied designs. Traditionally, it was worked to a garter-stitch finish (as in the Gibbie shawl — page 51), but a smoother effect is given if the non-pattern rows are worked in purl.

## OLD SHALE

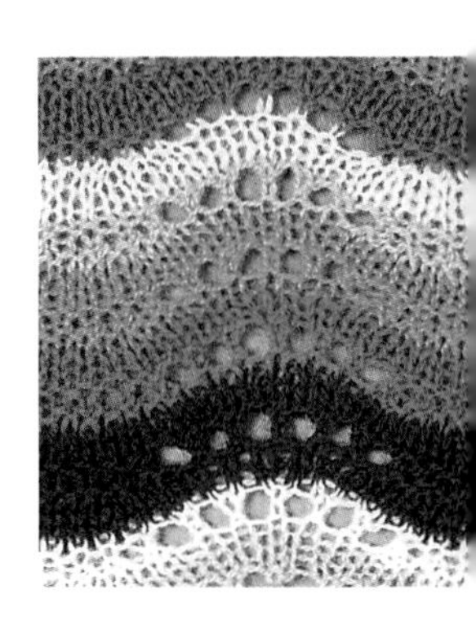

No. of stitches required — multiple of 18 No. of rows — 6

Starter Rows — Knit 2 rows, purl 1 row

Pattern row — (K1 T T T (c k1) 5 times, c T T T), repeat ( ) as required

Purl 1 row. Knit 3 rows. Purl 1 row.

Repeat pattern row and following 5 rows as required.

**NOTE**: The above is for working "in the round" — if the pattern is to be worked "on the straight" the sequence will be — pattern row, knit 1 row, purl 3 rows, knit 1 row.

This is one of the oldest Shetland stitch patterns and constantly used over the years. It was, and still is, used for the making of "haps", the traditional shawl worn by women of all ages as a very useful and warm garment. Often it was worn over the head and shoulders, crossed in front and tied behind the back to keep it in place while hands were left free for other occupations such as raising and carrying peats, all kinds of croft work, as well as knitting. It was not unusual for a small baby to be carried, safely wrapped in the securely fastened hap.

Traditionally it was worked in garter stitch and knitted in natural colours. The various patterns detailed in this book are worked in a slightly up-dated version of the original stitch pattern — knitted with less garter stitch and with stocking stitch substituted in part of the pattern.

The "hap" is a very versatile garment and many other shawl designs have been derived from it. It is wonderful for wrapping a baby to keep him or her cosy and useful for tucking in to pram or cot, as well as a really warm wrap for an adult.

As an accessory for keeping shoulders warm when driving, the author can recommend it!

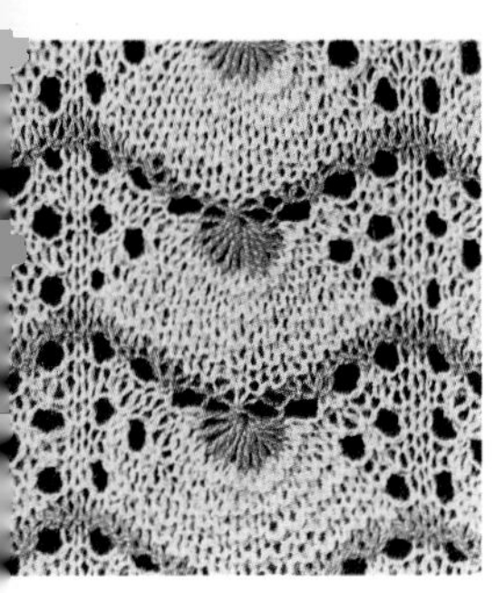

## COCKLESHELL

No. of stitches required — 19 | No. of rows — 12

In the following sequence 'k twice' is worked — knit into the front and back of the next stitch, which is the 'c' from the previous row.

Row 1 — K1, c T k13 T c k1 (19)

Row 2 — K1, k twice, k15, k twice, k1 (21)

Rows 3 and 4 — Knit

Row 5 — K1, c T c T, k11, T c T c, k1 (21)

Row 6 — K1, k twice, k1 k twice, k13, k twice k1 k twice, k1 (25)

Rows 7 and 8 — Knit

Row 9 — K1, c T c T c T (c k1) 11 times, c T c T c T c, k1 (37)

Row 10 — (k1, k twice) 3 times, slip next and every alternate stitch on to right-hand needle (13 sts.), at the same time dropping the 12 'c' stitches from the last row. Knit together the 13 sts. which were slipped, (k twice, k1) 3 times. (19)

Rows 11 and 12 — Knit

This is a pattern very much used for stoles and scarves, but can be used for other garments. It forms its own scalloped border and can be worked continuously as required.

It is recommended that additional edge stitches be worked at the beginning and end of rows, thus giving the garment a firm edge (3 stitches are sufficient for this).

## GRAFTING INSTRUCTIONS

Thread a wool needle with sufficient wool to suit the length of the required join, using wool remaining after working last row of knitting.

With wrong sides of work together and both needle points at the same end, pass the wool needle purlwise through the first stitch on the front needle (needle nearest to you) but do not slip stitch off, then pass the wool needle knitwise through the first stitch on the back needle, but do not slip stitch off. *** Pass wool needle knitwise through the first stitch on the front needle and slip off stitch, pass wool needle purlwise through next loop but do not slip off. Pass wool needle purlwise through stitch on back needle and slip off, then pass wool needle knitwise through next loop on back needle, but do not slip off. ***

Repeat sequence ***-*** until all stitches have been worked off. Fasten off securely.

## AFTER-CARE OF YOUR WORK

Always use lukewarm soapy water to wash your Shetland wool knitwear.

Rinse in lukewarm water and roll in a towel to absorb excess moisture.

Dry flat away from heat or sun, spread out to size and shape.

**NEVER** tumble-dry your Shetland wool garments. The 2-ply lace may be very gently spun, but the towelling method is recommended.

## BITS & PIECES — USEFUL ODD ITEMS

Knitting needle gauge

A few safety pins — about 1½″ long

Spare fine knitting needle

Fine wool needle — for cobweb

Wool needle — for 2-ply lace

Oddments of coloured wool for marking corner positions, etc.

# HINTS FOR WORKING WITH 1-PLY COBWEB LACE WOOL

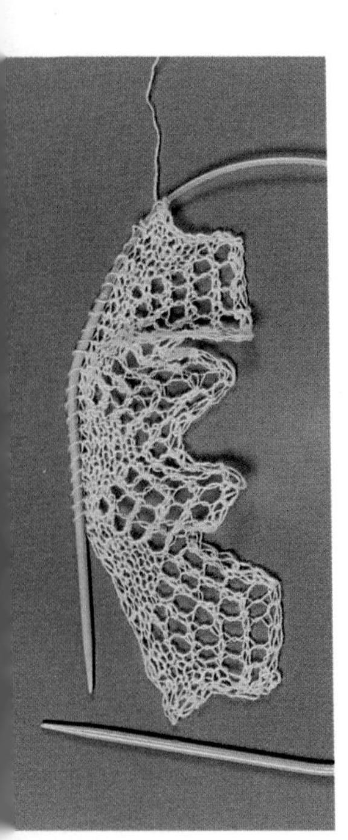

**Picking up stitches from border lace.**

1) When winding the wool it is helpful to use a "core" (a small amount of any wool loosely wound in to a soft ball) and wind the cobweb wool on to this very firmly, making a fairly solid ball. This will allow the "crinkle" to straighten out.

2) When knitting, a glass jam jar is ideal for keeping the ball of wool free-running but under control!

3) Most importantly — when knitting with cobweb wool always work with a fairly slack tension, on the needle size stated. Tight knitting does not allow the finished garment to dress into the correct size and shape and the intended lacy look.

4) When joining the wool, thread a very fine needle and splice into the fibre and twist the two thicknesses together — leave ends to be trimmed off AFTER dressing the garment.

5) It is a good idea to have available a very fine knitting needle (say, a size 13 or 14). Should you be unfortunate enough to need to take back any of the work, perhaps to rescue a dropped stitch, it is much easier to pick up the stitches with the finer needle, BUT, do remember to return to the correct needle before proceeding.

6) It is important to always slip purlwise the first stitch of every row of border lace as this makes it easier to pick up the stitches for the main part of the garment.

7) To keep one's place on the pattern — a hair-grip is most useful!

**NOTE:**

Scallops are worked **continuously** — stitches are **not** cast off after the last row of each scallop.

Where the instruction is to "work four times continuously" this means that the pattern as printed is worked four times to complete a round and so return to the "starter" stitch.

Spacer stitches are referred to in some of the stitch patterns. These are a number of knitted stitches to separate two motifs and thereby show them to the best advantage.

Tension is not quoted as all the garments are dressed when completed and the work is stretched to produce the approximate finished size.

# ABBREVIATIONS

| | | |
|---|---|---|
| K or k | — | Knit |
| P or p | — | Purl |
| st./sts. | — | Stitch/Stitches |
| T | — | "Take in" = knit 2 sts. together |
| 3T | — | "Take in 3" = knit 3 sts. together |
| TB | — | "Take in through back" = knit 2 sts. together through back loops |
| 3TB | — | "Take in 3 sts. through back" = knit 3 sts. together through back loops |
| PT | — | Purl 2 sts. together |
| PTB | — | Purl 2 sts. together through back loops |
| c | — | "Cast up" = wool forward |
| cT | — | Wool forward, knit 2 sts. together |
| cTB | — | Wool forward, knit 2 sts. together through back loops |
| Tc | — | Knit 2 sts. together, wool forward |
| cTc | — | Wool forward, knit 2 sts. together, wool forward |
| TcT | — | Knit 2 sts. together, wool forward, knit 2 sts. together |
| skp | — | Slip 1 stitch, knit 1, pass slipped stitch over |
| s2kp | — | Slip 2 stitches, knit 1, pass slipped stiches over |
| S1pw | — | Slip one stitch purlwise |
| S1kw | — | Slip one stitch knitwise |
| ( ) | — | Work instructions between brackets the number of times quoted |
| (22) | — | Figures in brackets at right-hand side of each row indicate the number of stitches remaining AFTER the row has been worked |
| ***-*** | — | Repeat from *** to *** |
| ....-.... | — | Dots used to separate one part of the row from the remainder — usually the centre panel is separated in this way. |

The abbreviations used vary from the usual "English" terms and offer the knitter the opportunity of working with some of the traditionally spoken Shetland terms. Many of these, to the author's knowledge, have not previously been published in any knitting book. Once learned, they are extremely simple to work with.

## NEEDLE SIZES

All needles used in these patterns are quoted in English and Metric. The following table is given for further reference.

### COMPARATIVE KNITTING NEEDLE SIZES

| BRITISH | 000 | 00 | 0 | 1 | 2 | 3 | 4 | 5 | 6 |
|---|---|---|---|---|---|---|---|---|---|
| METRIC (mm) | 9 | 8½ | 8 | 7½ | 7 | 6½ | 6 | 5½ | 5 |
| U.S.A. | 15 | 13 | — | 11 | 10½ | 10 | 9 | 8 | 7 |

| BRITISH | 7 | 8 | 9 | 10 | 11 | 12 | 13 | 14 |
|---|---|---|---|---|---|---|---|---|
| METRIC (mm) | 4½ | 4 | 3½ & 3¾ | 3¼ | 2¾&3 | 2½ | 2¼ | 2 |
| U.S.A. | 6 | 5 | 4 | 3 | 2 | 1 | 0 | 00 |

# *The Sheelagh Shawl*

## A FINE LACE SHAWL KNITTED IN 1-PLY COBWEB WOOL

**Size — 56'' x 56'' (140cm x 140cm)**

**MATERIALS** : 10 hanks — 1-ply cobweb lace wool
1 circular needle — size 11 (3.00mm) — 30" (80cm) long
1 circular needle — size 11 (3.00mm) — 24" (60cm) long
5 double-ended needles — size 12 (2.75mm)

This shawl is designed as a ladies' evening shawl or for a baby's christening. The next pattern is for a matching christening robe.

The shawl includes Miniature Leaf stitch, Horseshoe stitch and Shetland Fern patterns as well as Print of the Wave pattern in the main border.

The main part of the shawl is knitted on the 30" No.11 circular needle. Towards the centre it will be necessary to change to the 24" needle in order not to stretch the work unduly. After Row 177 the work is continued on the 5 double-ended No.12 needles.

The border is made up of the combined Print of the Wave and Five Hole Border Lace as shown in the 48 row detail on the next page.

**These 48 rows form four patterns of Print of the Wave stitch and three scallops,** and are worked continuously (40 times), until 160 patterns of Print of the Wave and 120 scallops have been completed. Graft together the cast-on stitches and the stitches from the last row of the border lace.

**NOTE** : 120 scallops produce 960 stitches equalling 240 stitches per side.

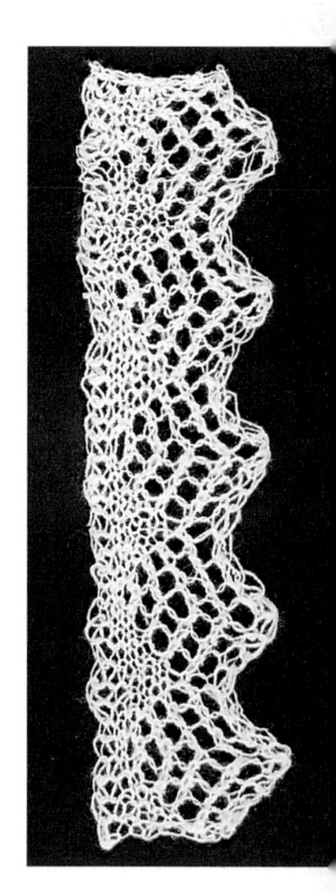

*The Sheelagh Shawl*

**PRINT OF THE WAVE & FIVE HOLE BORDER LACE** : With No.11 needle cast on 33 stitches **VERY** loosely.

| | | | |
|---|---|---|---|
| **1st and every alternate row : S1pw k1, purl 21, knit to end.** | | | (33) |
| 2nd Row : | S1pw k1 cTc, k6 ........................ | Tc Tc Tc, k1 T k3 T k1, c k1 c, Tc Tc k3 | (34) |
| 4th Row : | S1pw k1 (cT) twice, c k5 ........ | Tc Tc Tc, k1 T k1 T k1, c k3 c, Tc Tc k3 | (35) |
| 6th Row : | S1pw k1 (cT) 3 times, c k4 .... | Tc Tc Tc, k1 s2kp k1, c k5 c, Tc Tc k3 | (36) |
| 8th Row : | S1pw k1 (cT) 4 times, c k3 .... | k1 cT cT, c k1 c, k1 T k3 T k1, cT cT cT k2 | (37) |
| 10th Row : | S1pw T (cT) 4 times, k3 .......... | k1 cT cT, c k3 c, k1 T k1 T k1, cT cT cT k2 | (36) |
| 12th Row : | S1pw T (cT) 3 times, k4 .......... | k1 cT cT, c k5 c, k1 s2kp k1, cT cT cT k2 | (35) |
| 14th Row : | S1pw T (cT) twice, k5 .............. | Tc Tc Tc, k1 T k3 T k1, c k1 c, Tc Tc k3 | (34) |
| 16th Row : | S1pw TcT, k6 ............................ | Tc Tc Tc, k1 T k1 T k1, c k3 c, Tc Tc k3 | (33) |
| 18th Row : | S1pw k1 cTc, k6 ........................ | Tc Tc Tc, k1 s2kp k1, c k5 c, Tc Tc k3 | (34) |
| 20th Row : | S1pw k1 (cT) twice, c k5 ........ | k1 cT cT, c k1 c, k1 T k3 T k1, cT cT cT k2 | (35) |
| 22nd Row : | S1pw k1 (cT) 3 times, c k4 .... | k1 cT cT, c k3 c, k1 T k1 T k1, cT cT cT k2 | (36) |
| 24th Row : | S1pw k1 (cT) 4 times, c k3 .... | k1 cT cT, c k5 c, k1 s2kp k1, cT cT cT k2 | (37) |
| 26th Row : | S1pw T (cT) 4 times, k3 .......... | Tc Tc Tc, k1 T k3 T k1, c k1 c, Tc Tc k3 | (36) |
| 28th Row : | S1pw T (cT) 3 times, k4 .......... | Tc Tc Tc, k1 T k1 T k1, c k3 c, Tc Tc k3 | (35) |
| 30th Row : | S1pw T (cT) twice, k5 .............. | Tc Tc Tc, k1 s2kp k1, c k5 c, Tc Tc k3 | (34) |
| 32nd Row : | S1pw TcT, k6 ............................ | k1 cT cT, c k1 c, k1 T k3 T k1, cT cT cT k2 | (33) |
| 34th Row : | S1pw k1 cTc, k6 ........................ | k1 cT cT, c k3 c, k1 T k1 T k1, cT cT cT k2 | (34) |
| 36th Row : | S1pw k1 (cT) twice, c k5 ........ | k1 cT cT, c k5 c, k1 s2kp k1, cT cT cT k2 | (35) |
| 38th Row : | S1pw k1 (cT) 3 times, c k4 .... | Tc Tc Tc, k1 T k3 T k1, c k1 c, Tc Tc k3 | (36) |
| 40th Row : | S1pw k1 (cT) 4 times, c k3 .... | Tc Tc Tc, k1 T k1 T k1, c k3 c, Tc Tc k3 | (37) |
| 42nd Row : | S1pw T (cT) 4 times, k3 .......... | Tc Tc Tc, k1 s2kp k1, c k5 c, Tc Tc k3 | (36) |
| 44th Row : | S1pw T (cT) 3 times, k4 .......... | k1 cT cT, c k1 c, k1 T k3 T k1, cT cT cT k2 | (35) |
| 46th Row : | S1pw T (cT) twice, k5 .............. | k1 cT cT, c k3 c, k1 T k1 T k1, cT cT cT k2 | (34) |
| 48th Row : | S1pw TcT, k6 ............................ | k1 cT cT, c k5 c, k1 s2kp k1, cT cT cT k2 | (33) |

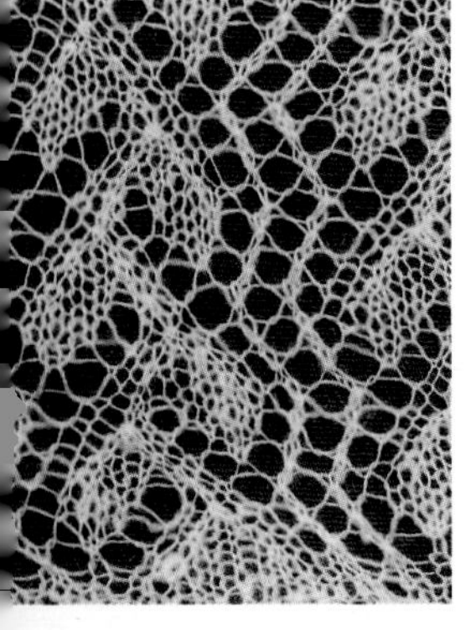

**From border lace — pick up 960 stitches, and (knit 240 sts. through back loops) 4 times, putting in marker threads at the end of each 240 sts. (i.e. at the four corners).** Additional marker threads in a different colour may be placed at the centre of each side to aid working if required.

**NOTE** : From now on instructions are given for **ONE SIDE ONLY** to be worked **FOUR TIMES CONTINUOUSLY,** up to and including Row 223.

| | |
|---|---|
| **Next row — Purl** | **(240)** |
| **Next row — T, knit 117, T, knit 117, TB.** | **(237)** |
| **Purl one row.** | **(237)** |

**ROW**

| | | |
|---|---|---|
| 1 | T k6 (Tc k1 cTB k7) 18 times, Tc k1 cTB, k6 TB | (235) |
| **2** | **and every alternate row — knit** | |
| 3 | T k4 (Tc k3 cTB k5) 18 times, Tc k3 cTB, k4 TB | (233) |
| 5 | T k4 (cTB k1 Tc k7) 18 times, cTB k1 Tc, k4 TB | (231) |
| 7 | T k4 (c S2kp c k9) 18 times, c s2kp c, k4 TB | (229) |
| 9 | T k225 TB | (227) |
| 11 | T k7 (Tc k1 cTB k7) 17 times, Tc k1 cTB, k7 TB | (225) |
| 13 | T k5 (Tc k3 cTB k5) 17 times, Tc k3 cTB, k5 TB | (223) |
| 15 | T k5 (cTB k1 Tc k7) 17 times, cTB k1 Tc, k5 TB | (221) |
| 17 | T k5 (c s2kp c k9) 17 times, c s2kp c, k5 TB | (219) |
| 19 | T k215 TB | (217) |
| 21 | T k213 TB | (215) |
| 22 | Knit | |

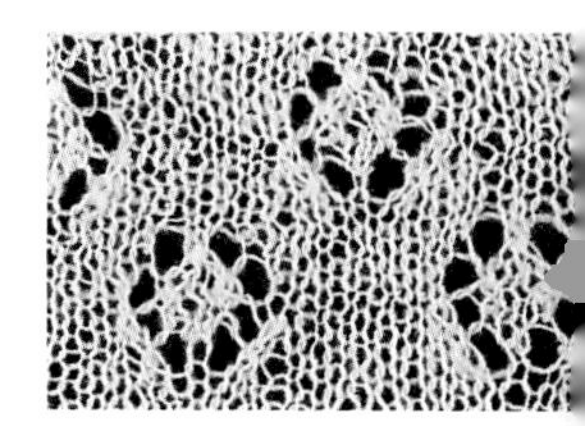

# *The Sheelagh Shawl*

**MINIATURE LEAF STITCH**

| ROW | | |
|---|---|---|
| 23 | T k3 (k1 Tc k1 cTB) 34 times, k4 TB | (213) |
| 25 | T k1 (c s2kp c k3) 34 times, c s2kp c k1 TB | (211) |
| 27 | T k2 cTB (k1 Tc k1 cTB) 33 times, k1 Tc k2 TB | (209) |
| 29 | T k2 (c s2kp c k3) 33 times, c s2kp c k2 TB | (207) |
| 31 | T k3 cTB (k1 Tc k1 cTB) 32 times, k1 Tc k3 TB | (205) |
| 33 | T k3 (c s2kp c k3) 33 times, TB | (203) |
| 35 | T (k1 Tc k1 cTB) 33 times, k1 TB | (201) |
| 37 | T k4 (c s2kp c k3) 32 times, k1 TB | (199) |
| 39 | T k1 (k1 Tc k1 cTB) 32 times, k2 TB | (197) |
| 41 | T, Tc k3 (c s2kp c k3) 31 times, cTB, TB | (195) |
| 43 | Tc TB (k1 Tc k1 cTB) 31 times, k1 Tc TB | (193) |
| 45 | T (c s2kp c k3) 31 times, c s2kp c TB | (191) |
| 47 | T k1 cTB (k1 Tc k1 cTB) 30 times, k1 Tc k1 TB | (189) |
| 49 | T k2 Tc k3 (c s2kp c k3) 29 times, cT k2 TB | (187) |
| 51 | T k2 cTB (k1 Tc k1 cTB) 29 times, k1 Tc k2 TB | (185) |
| 53 | T k2 (c s2kp c k3) 29 times, c s2kp c k2 TB | (183) |
| 55 | T k179 TB | (181) |
| 57 | T k177 TB | (179) |
| 59 | T k175 TB | (177) |
| 60 | Knit | |

**HORSESHOE STITCH**

| | | |
|---|---|---|
| 61 | T k1 T (k3 c k1 c k3 s2kp) 16 times, k3 c k1 c k3, TB k1 TB | (175) |
| 63 | T, T (k2 c k3 c k2 s2kp) 16 times, k2 c k3 c k2, TB, TB | (173) |
| 65 | T, T c k5 c k1 s2kp (k1 c k5 c k1 s2kp) 15 times, k1 c k5 c, TB, TB | (171) |
| 67 | T k7 c s2kp (c k7 c s2kp) 15 times, c k7 TB | (169) |
| 69 | T k3 c k3 s2kp (k3 c k1 c k3 s2kp) 15 times, k3 c k3 TB | (167) |

| ROW | | |
|---|---|---|
| 71 | T k3 c k2 s2kp (k2 c k3 c k2 s2kp) 15 times, k2 c k3 TB | (165) |
| 73 | T k3 c k1 s2kp (k1 c k5 c k1 s2kp) 15 times, k1 c k3 TB | (163) |
| 75 | T k3 c s2kp (c k7 c s2kp) 15 times, c k3 TB | (161) |
| 77 | T k3 T (k3 c k1 c k3 s2kp) 14 times, k3 c k1 c k3, TB k3 TB | (159) |
| 79 | T k2 T (k2 c k3 c k2 s2kp) 14 times, k2 c k3 c k2, TB k2 TB | (157) |
| 81 | T k1 T (k1 c k5 c k1 s2kp) 14 times, k1 c k5 c k1, TB k1 TB | (155) |
| 83 | T, T (c k7 c s2kp) 14 times, c k7 c, TB, TB | (153) |
| 85 | T k5 c k3 s2kp (k3 c k1 c k3 s2kp) 13 times, k3 c k5 TB | (151) |
| 87 | T k5 c k2 s2kp (k2 c k3 c k2 s2kp) 13 times, k2 c k5 TB | (149) |
| 89 | T k5 c k1 s2kp (k1 c k5 c k1 s2kp) 13 times, k1 c k5 TB | (147) |
| 91 | T k5 c s2kp (c k7 c s2kp) 13 times, c k5 TB | (145) |
| 93 | T k141 TB | (143) |
| 95 | T k139 TB | (141) |
| 96 | Knit | |

**MINIATURE LEAF STITCH**

| | | |
|---|---|---|
| 97 | T k2 (k1 Tc k1 cTB) 22 times, k3 TB | (139) |
| 99 | T k1 Tc k3 (c s2kp c k3) 21 times, cTB k1 TB | (137) |
| 101 | T k1 cTB (k1 Tc k1 cTB) 21 times, k1 Tc k1 TB | (135) |
| 103 | T k1 (c s2kp c k3) 21 times, c s2kp c k1 TB | (133) |
| 105 | T k2 cTB (k1 Tc k1 cTB) 20 times, k1 Tc k2 TB | (131) |
| 107 | T k2 (c s2kp c k3) 20 times, c s2kp c k2 TB | (129) |
| 109 | T, Tc k1 cTB (k1 Tc k1 cTB) 20 times, TB | (127) |
| 111 | T k3 (c s2kp c k3) 20 times, TB | (125) |

**NOTE** : The following pattern rows consist of three parts; the beginning, the centre which is separated by dots and the end. **ROWS 128, 130, 146 & 148 are NOT knit rows, and are detailed.**

**MINIATURE LEAF & FERN SEQUENCE**

**ROW**

113 T (k1 Tc k1 cTB) 3 times, k1 Tc k1, k33....Tc k1 cTB k1 Tc k1 cTB....
k33, k1 cTB (k1 Tc k1 cTB) 3 times, k1 TB (123)

115 T k4 (c s2kp c k3) twice, c s2kp c k2, k32....Tc k3 c s2kp c k3 cTB....
k32, k2 (c s2kp c k3) twice, c s2kp c, k4 TB (121)

117 T k2 Tc k1 cTB (k1 Tc k1 cTB) twice, k1, k7 c skp k16, c skp k6
....cTB k1 Tc k1 cTB k1 Tc....k7 c skp k16, c skp k6 (k1 Tc k1 cTB) 3 times, k2 TB (119)

119 T, TB c k3 (c s2kp c k3) twice, cTB k5 Tc k1 cTB, k13, Tc k1 cTB k5,
....k1 c s2kp c k3 c s2kp c k1....
k5 Tc k1 cTB, k13, Tc k1 cTB k5, Tc k3 (c s2kp c k3) twice, cTB, TB (117)

121 Tc TB (k1 Tc k1 cTB) twice, k1 Tc k1, k4 Tc k3 cTB, k11, Tc k3 cTB, k4
....Tc k1 cTB k1 Tc k1 cTB....
k4 Tc k3 cTB, k11, Tc k3 cTB, k4, k1 cTB (k1 Tc k1 cTB) twice, k1 Tc TB (115)

123 T (c s2kp c k3) 3 times, k3 cTB c s2kp c Tc, k11, cTB c s2kp c Tc k3
....TB c k3 c s2kp c k3 cT....
k3 cTB c s2kp c Tc, k11, cTB c s2kp c Tc k3 (k3 c s2kp c) 3 times, TB (113)

125 T k1 cTB (k1 Tc k1 cTB) twice, k3 Tc k1 cTB k1, Tc k1 cTB k7, Tc k1 cTB k1,
Tc k1 cTB....k2 cTB k1 Tc k1 cTB k1 Tc k2....Tc k1 cTB k1,
Tc k1 cTB k7, Tc k1 cTB k1, Tc k1 cTB k3 Tc k1 cTB k1, Tc k1 cTB k1, Tc k1 TB (111)

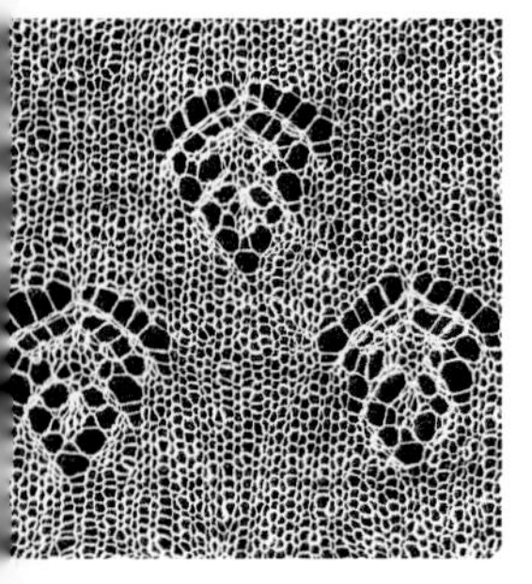

127 T k1 (c s2kp c k3) twice, cTB k2, cTB cTB k3 Tc Tc, k7, cTB cTB k3 Tc Tc
....k3 (c s2kp c k3) twice....
cTB cTB k3 Tc Tc, k7, cTB cTB k3 Tc Tc k2 Tc (k3 c s2kp c) twice, k1 TB (109)

**128** K16, k3, cTB cTB k1 Tc Tc, k9, cTB cTB k1 Tc Tc, k3....k11....
k3, cTB cTB k1 Tc Tc, k9, cTB cTB k1 Tc Tc, k3, k16 (109)

129 T k2 (cTB k1 Tc k1) twice, k4 cTB c s2kp c Tc, k11, cTB c s2kp c Tc k4
....Tc k1 cTB k1 Tc k1 cTB....
k4 cTB c s2kp c Tc, k11, cTB c s2kp c Tc k4 (k1 cTB k1 Tc) twice, k2 TB (107)

| ROW | | |
|---|---|---|
| **130** | K15, k5 cTB k1 Tc, k13, cTB k1 Tc k5....k11....k5 cTB k1 Tc, k13, cTB k1 Tc k5, k15 | (107) |
| 131 | T k2 (c s2kp c k3) twice, k5 c s2kp c, k15, c s2kp c k5....TB c k3 c s2kp c k3 cT.... k5 c s2kp c, k15, c s2kp c k5 (k3 c s2kp c) twice, k2 TB | (105) |
| 133 | T (T c k1 cTB k1) twice, k33....cTB k1 Tc k1 cTB k1 Tc....k33 (k1 Tc k1 cTB) twice, TB | (103) |
| 135 | T k3 c s2kp c k3 cTB k9, k7 c skp k6, k9....k1 c s2kp c k3 c s2kp c k1.... k9, k7 c skp k6, k9 Tc k3 c s2kp c, k3 TB | (101) |
| 137 | T k1 Tc k1 cTB k1 Tc k1, k14 Tc k1 cTB k14....Tc k1 cTB k1 Tc k1 cTB.... k14 Tc k1 cTB k14, k1 cTB k1 Tc k1 cTB, k1 TB | (99) |
| 139 | T k4 c s2kp c k3, k12 Tc k3 cTB k12....Tc k3 c s2kp c k3 cTB.... k12 Tc k3 cTB k12, k3 c s2kp c, k4 TB | (97) |
| 141 | T k2 (Tc k1 cTB k1) twice, k7 cTB c s2kp c Tc k7....cTB (k1 Tc k1 cTB) 3 times, k1 Tc.... k7 cTB c s2kp c Tc k7 (k1 Tc k1 cTB) twice, k2 TB | (95) |
| 143 | T, TB c k3 c s2kp c k3 cTB k5, Tc k1 cTB k1 Tc k1 cTB k5 ....k1 (c s2kp c k3) 3 times, c s2kp c k1.... k5 Tc k1 cTB k1 Tc k1 cTB k5, Tc k3 c s2kp c k3 cTB, TB | (93) |
| 145 | T (cTB k1 Tc k1) twice, k5 cTB cTB k3 Tc Tc k5....Tc k1 cTB (k1 Tc k1 cTB) 3 times.... K5 cTB cTB k3 Tc Tc k5 (k1 cTB k1 Tc) twice, TB | (91) |
| **146** | K13, k6 cTB cTB k1 Tc Tc k6....k23....k6 cTB cTB k1 Tc Tc k6, k13 | (91) |
| 147 | T c s2kp c k3 c s2kp c k2, k7 cTB c s2kp c Tc k7....k4 (c s2kp c k3) 3 times, k1.... k7 cTB c s2kp c Tc k7, k2 c s2kp c k3 c s2kp c, TB | (89) |
| **148** | K12, k8 cTB k1 Tc k8....k23....k8 cTB k1 Tc k8, k12 | (89) |
| 149 | T k1 cTB k1 Tc k1 cTB k1, k9 c s2kp c k9....cTB (k1 Tc k1 cTB) 3 times, k1 Tc.... k9 c s2kp c k9, k1 Tc k1 cTB k1 Tc k1, TB | (87) |
| 151 | T k1 c s2kp c k3 cTB, k21....k1 (c s2kp c k3) 3 times, c s2kp c k1....k21, Tc k3 c s2kp c, k1 TB | (85) |
| 153 | T k2 cTB k1 Tc k1, k21....Tc k1 cTB (k1 Tc k1 cTB) 3 times....k21, k1 cTB k1 Tc, k2 TB | (83) |
| 155 | T k2 c s2kp c k2, k20....TB c (k3 c s2kp c) 3 times, k3 cT....k20, k2 c s2kp c, k2 TB | (81) |
| 156 | Knit | |

**END OF FERN SEQUENCE**

| ROW | | |
|---|---|---|
| 157 | T, T c k1 cTB (k1 Tc k1 cTB) 12 times, TB | (79) |
| 159 | T k3 (c s2kp c k3) 12 times, TB | (77) |
| 161 | T (k1 Tc k1 cTB) 12 times, k1 TB | (75) |
| 163 | T k4 (c s2kp c k3) 10 times, c s2kp c, k4 TB | (73) |
| 165 | T k69 TB | (71) |
| 167 | T k67 TB | (69) |
| 169 | T k6, TB c k1 cT, k5 (TB c k1 cT k9) twice, TB c k1 cT, k5, TB c k1 cT, k6 TB | (67) |
| 171 | T k4, TB c k3 cT, k3 (TB c k3 cT k7) twice, TB c k3 cT, k3, TB c k3 cT, k4 TB | (65) |
| 173 | T k4, cTB k1 Tc k5 (cTB k1 Tc k9) twice, cTB k1 Tc k5, cTB k1 Tc, k4 TB | (63) |
| 175 | T k4, c s2kp c k7 (c s2kp c k11) twice, c s2kp c k7, c s2kp c, k4 TB | (61) |
| 177 | T k7, TB c k1 cT k9, TB c k1 cT k5, TB c k1 cT k9, TB c k1 cT k7, TB | (59) |

**CHANGE TO No. 12 NEEDLES**

| | | |
|---|---|---|
| 178 | Knit | |
| 179 | T k5, TB c k3 cT k7, TB c k3 cT k3, TB c k3 cT k7, TB c k3 cT, k5 TB | (57) |
| 181 | T k5, cTB k1 Tc k9, cTB k1 Tc k5, cTB k1 Tc k9, cTB k1 Tc, k5 TB | (55) |
| 183 | T k5, c s2kp c k11, c s2kp c k7, c s2kp c k11, c s2kp c, k5 TB | (53) |
| 185 | T k12 (TB c k1 cT k5) twice, TB c k1 cT, k12 TB | (51) |
| 187 | T k10 (TB c k3 cT k3) twice, TB c k3 cT, k10 TB | (49) |
| 189 | T k10 (cTB k1 Tc k5) twice, cTB k1 Tc, k10 TB | (47) |
| 191 | T k10 (c s2kp c k7) twice, c s2kp c, k10 TB | (45) |
| 193 | T k13, TB c k1 cT k5, TB c k1 cT, k13 TB | (43) |
| 195 | T k11, TB c k3 cT k3, TB c k3 cT, k11 TB | (41) |
| 197 | T k11, cTB k1 Tc k5, cTB k1 Tc, k11 TB | (39) |
| 199 | T k11, c s2kp c k7, c s2kp c, k11 TB | (37) |
| 201 | T k4 (TB c k1 cT k5) twice, TB c k1 cT, k4 TB | (35) |
| 203 | T k2 (TB c k3 cT k3) twice, TB c k3 cT, k2 TB | (33) |
| 205 | T k2 (cTB k1 Tc k5) twice, cTB k1 Tc, k2 TB | (31) |

| ROW | | |
|---|---|---|
| 207 | T k2 (c s2kp c k7) twice, c s2kp c, k2 TB | (29) |
| 209 | T k5 (TB c k1 cT k5) twice, TB | (27) |
| 211 | T k3 (TB c k3 cT k3) twice, TB | (25) |
| 213 | T k1 TB, cTB k1 Tc, T k1 TB, cTB k1 Tc, T, k1 TB | (19) |
| 215 | T k2, c s2kp c, T k1 TB, c s2kp c, k2 TB | (15) |
| 216 | Knit | (15) |
| 217 | T k11 TB | (13) |
| 218 | Knit | (13) |
| 219 | T k2, TB c k1 cT, k2 TB | (11) |
| 220 | Knit | (11) |
| 221 | T, TB c k3 cT, TB | (9) |
| 222 | Knit | (9) |
| 223 | T, cTB k1 Tc, TB | (7) |

**Working continuously,** k27, TB (k1 c s2kp c k1 TB) 3 times,
k1 c s2kp c k1, k24, k24, (TB) 12 times.

**DRAW UP LOOSELY AND FASTEN OFF SECURELY**

**TO DRESS SHAWL :** Wash **BY HAND ONLY** in lukewarm soapy water, squeezing gently. Rinse in lukewarm water. Roll up in a towel to absorb excess moisture. Stretch out to dry to a perfect square 56" x 56" approx., away from heat or sun, on a shawl frame or pin out scallops at points on to a white sheet, and dry flat.

# *The Sheelagh Robe*

## A FINE LACE CHRISTENING ROBE KNITTED IN 1-PLY COBWEB WOOL

### Size — TO FIT BABY UP TO 6 MONTHS

**MATERIALS** : 7 hanks — 1-ply cobweb lace wool
1 circular needle — size 11 (3.00mm) — 24" (60cm) long
1 circular needle — size 12 (2.75mm) — 16" (40cm) long
Nylon press fasteners for back opening
Ribbon for sleeve cuffs and other decoration if required

This christening robe is designed to match the shawl in the preceding chapter. The lower part of the robe features a double layer border of Print of the Wave and Five Hole Border Lace.

As well as including the stitch patterns used for the shawl, Bird's Eye stitch is introduced for the yoke. This is a very useful stretchy stitch pattern and therefore suitable for a garment intended for an infant — it makes for easier dressing!

**WORKING INSTRUCTIONS** :

**THE UPPER BORDER** comprises of one pattern of PRINT OF THE WAVE & FIVE HOLE BORDER LACE.

With No. 11 Needle cast on **33 sts.** **VERY** loosely, and work the 48 rows of the pattern, on the following page, 10 times (480 rows).

Graft the cast-on stitches together with those left on the needle.
With right side of work facing and starting at join (centre back), pick up 240 sts. along straight edge.
Knit one row through back loops. Knit a further 3 rows.
Leave these stitches on a spare needle and proceed with the lower border.

**THE LOWER BORDER** comprises of **two** patterns of PRINT OF THE WAVE & FIVE HOLE BORDER LACE.

With No. 11 Needle cast on **47** sts. **VERY** loosely, and work the 48 rows of the pattern, on the following page, 10 times (480 rows).

Graft the cast on stitches together with those left on the needle.
With right side of work facing and starting at join (centre back), pick up 240 sts. along straight edge.
Knit one row through back loops. Knit a further 3 rows.

(continued overleaf).

## *The Sheelagh Robe*

**NOTE** : This pattern sequence is detailed for either the upper **OR** lower border.

**PRINT OF THE WAVE & FIVE HOLE BORDER LACE**

**1st and every alternate row : S1pw k1, purl 21 OR purl 35, knit to end.**

2nd Row : S1pw k1 cTc, k6 ...................... Tc Tc Tc (k1 T k3 T k1, c k1 c, Tc Tc) OR twice, k3 (34/48)

4th Row : S1pw k1 (cT) twice, c k5 ........ Tc Tc Tc (k1 T k1 T k1, c k3 c, Tc Tc) OR twice, k3 (35/49)

6th Row : S1pw k1 (cT) 3 times, c k4 .... Tc Tc Tc (k1 s2kp k1, c k5 c, Tc Tc) OR twice, k3 (36/50)

8th Row : S1pw k1 (cT) 4 times, c k3 ....... k1 cT cT (c k1 c, k1 T k3 T k1, cT cT) OR twice, cT k2 (37/51)

10th Row : S1pw T (cT) 4 times, k3 ............ k1 cT cT (c k3 c, k1 T k1 T k1, cT cT) OR twice, cT k2 (36/50)

12th Row : S1pw T (cT) 3 times, k4 .......... k1 cT cT (c k5 c, k1 s2kp k1, cT cT) OR twice, cT k2 (35/49)

14th Row : S1pw T (cT) twice, k5 ............. Tc Tc Tc (k1 T k3 T k1, c k1 c, Tc Tc) OR twice, k3 (34/48)

16th Row : S1pw TcT, k6 ............................ Tc Tc Tc (k1 T k1 T k1, c k3 c, Tc Tc) OR twice, k3 (33/47)

18th Row : S1pw k1 cTc, k6 ....................... Tc Tc Tc (k1 s2kp k1, c k5 c, Tc Tc) OR twice, k3 (34/48)

20th Row : S1pw k1 (cT) twice, c k5 .......... k1 cT cT (c k1 c, k1 T k3 T k1, cT cT) OR twice, cT k2 (35/49)

22nd Row : S1pw k1 (cT) 3 times, c k4 ...... k1 cT cT (c k3 c, k1 T k1 T k1, cT cT) OR twice, cT k2 (36/50)

24th Row : S1pw k1 (cT) 4 times, c k3 .... k1 cT cT (c k5 c, k1 s2kp k1, cT cT) OR twice, cT k2 (37/51)

26th Row : S1pw T (cT) 4 times, k3 .......... Tc Tc Tc (k1 T k3 T k1, c k1 c, Tc Tc) OR twice, k3 (36/50)

28th Row : S1pw T (cT) 3 times, k4 .......... Tc Tc Tc (k1 T k1 T k1, c k3 c, Tc Tc) OR twice, k3 (35/49)

30th Row : S1pw T (cT) twice, k5 ............. Tc Tc Tc (k1 s2kp k1, c k5 c, Tc Tc) OR twice, k3 (34/48)

32nd Row : S1pw TcT, k6 ............................ k1 cT cT (c k1 c, k1 T k3 T k1, cT cT) OR twice, cT k2 (33/47)

34th Row : S1pw k1 cTc, k6 ......................... k1 cT cT (c k3 c, k1 T k1 T k1, cT cT) OR twice, cT k2 (34/48)

36th Row : S1pw k1 (cT) twice, c k5 ........ k1 cT cT (c k5 c, k1 s2kp k1, cT cT) OR twice, cT k2 (35/49)

38th Row : S1pw k1 (cT) 3 times, c k4 .... Tc Tc Tc (k1 T k3 T k1, c k1 c, Tc Tc) OR twice, k3 (36/50)

40th Row : S1pw k1 (cT) 4 times, c k3 .... Tc Tc Tc (k1 T k1 T k1, c k3 c, Tc Tc) OR twice, k3 (37/51)

42nd Row : S1pw T (cT) 4 times, k3 ......... Tc Tc Tc (k1 s2kp k1, c k5 c, Tc Tc) OR twice, k3 (36/50)

44th Row : S1pw T (cT) 3 times, k4 ............ k1 cT cT (c k1 c, k1 T k3 T k1, cT cT) OR twice, cT k2 (35/49)

46th Row : S1pw T (cT) twice, k5 ................ k1 cT cT (c k3 c, k1 T k1 T k1, cT cT) OR twice, cT k2 (34/48)

48th Row : S1pw TcT, k6 ............................ k1 cT cT (c k5 c, k1 s2kp k1, cT cT) OR twice, cT k2 (33/47)

**These 48 rows form four patterns of Print of the Wave stitch and three scallops,** and are worked continuously (10 times), until 40 patterns of Print of the Wave stitch and 30 scallops have been completed. 30 scallops produce 240 stitches.

**THE LOWER BORDER INSTRUCTIONS** (continued).

Mark starter stitch with a coloured thread.
Work the 8 rows of the Miniature Leaf stitch sequence, 5 times, (40 rows).

**MINIATURE LEAF STITCH SEQUENCE**

**ROW**

1 (K1 cTB k1 Tc) repeat to end of row.

2 Knit 240

3 K2 c s2kp c (k3 c s2kp c) repeat ( — ) to last st., k1

4 Knit 240

5 (K1 Tc k1 cTB) repeat to end of row.

6 Knit **239 sts. ONLY** --- the last stitch is required for the s2kp at start of next row.

7 (S2kp c k3 c) repeat to end of row.

8 Knit 240

Knit a further 4 rows.

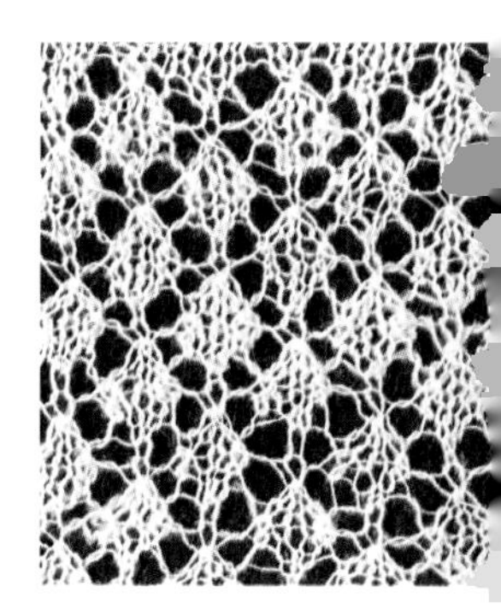

**TO JOIN THE TWO BORDERS** : Place the wrong side of the UPPER BORDER to the right side of the LOWER BORDER, and with **BOTH** right sides facing you, knit one row taking together one stitch from each border, and continue until all the stitches from both borders have been worked.
Mark starter stitch with a coloured thread, and knit a further 2 rows. (240 sts.)

Continue with :
**ROUNDEL STITCH SEQUENCE**

**ROW**

1 K4 (Tc k1 cTB k7) 19 times, Tc k1 cTB k3

**2 and every alternate row — knit 240**

3 K3 (Tc k3 cTB k5) 19 times, Tc k3 cTB k2

5 K4 (cTB k1 Tc k7) 19 times, cTB k1 Tc k3

7 K5 (c s2kp c k9) 19 times, c s2kp c k4

8 Knit 240

Knit a further row of 240 sts.
Next row — Knit **234 sts. ONLY**

Work a second 8 row sequence of the Roundel stitch pattern (the Roundels will be positioned in the centre of the stocking stitch spaces of the first sequence).
**Knit a further 6 stitches,** so returning to the centre back and marked centre stitch.

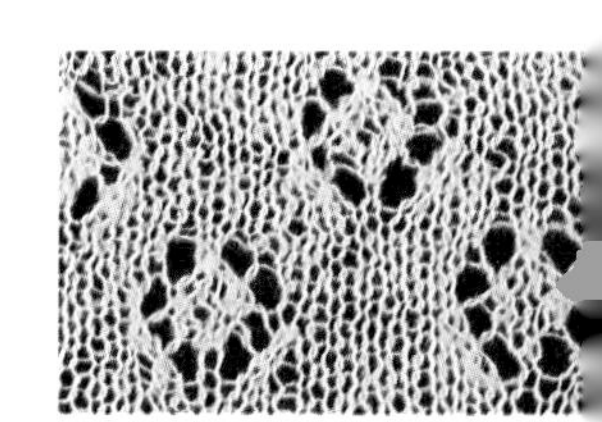

**WORKING INSTRUCTIONS** (continued).

Knit 4 rows

Continue, working the 8 rows of the Miniature Leaf stitch sequence, 3 times, (24 rows).

**MINIATURE LEAF STITCH SEQUENCE**

**ROW**

1 (K1 cTB k1 Tc) repeat to end of row.

2 Knit 240

3 K2 c s2kp c (k3 c s2kp c) repeat ( — ) to last st., k1

4 Knit 240

5 (K1 Tc k1 cTB) repeat to end of row.

6 Knit **239 sts. ONLY** --- the last stitch is required for the s2kp at start of next row.

7 (S2kp c k3 c) repeat to end of row.

8 Knit 240

Knit a further 4 rows.

Continue, working the 8 rows of the Horseshoe stitch sequence, 3 times, (24 rows).

**HORSESHOE STITCH SEQUENCE**

**ROW**

1 K1 (c k3 s2kp k3 c k1) 23 times, c k3 s2kp k3 c

2 Knit 240

3 K2 (c k2 s2kp k2 c k3) 23 times, c k2 s2kp k2 c k1

4 Knit 240

5 K3 (c k1 s2kp k1 c k5) 23 times, c k1 s2kp k1 c k2

6 Knit 240

7 K4 (c s2kp c k7) 23 times, c s2kp c k3

8 Knit 240

Knit a further 4 rows.

Continue, working the 8 rows of the Miniature Leaf stitch sequence, twice, (16 rows).

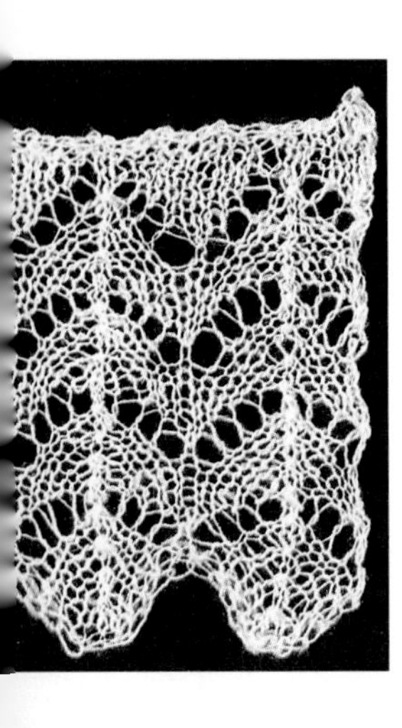

Continue with :
**MINIATURE LEAF & TWO-FERN SEQUENCE**

**ROW**

1 K1 cTB k1 Tc k1 cTB *** k31 (Tc K1 cTB K1) twice, Tc k1 cTB ***
work *** — *** 4 times in all, k31, Tc k1 cTB k1 Tc

2 Knit 240 (whole row)

3 K2 c s2kp c k3 cTB *** k29, Tc (k3 c s2kp c) twice, k3 cTB ***
work *** — *** 4 times in all, k29, Tc k3 c s2kp c k1

4 Knit 240

5 K1 Tc k1 cTB k1 Tc *** k7 c skp k14 c skp k6 (cTB k1 Tc k1) twice, cTB k1 Tc ***
work *** — *** 4 times in all, k7 c skp k14 c skp k6, cTB k1 Tc k1 cTB

6 **Knit 239 sts. ONLY** --- the last stitch is required for the s2kp at start of next row.

7 S2kp c k3 c s2kp c k1 *** k5 Tc k1 cTB k11 Tc k1 cTB k5, k1 (c s2kp c k3) twice, c s2kp c k1 ***
work *** — *** 4 times in all, k5 Tc k1 cTB k11 Tc k1 cTB k5, k1 c s2kp c k3 c

8 Knit 240

9 K1 cTB k1 Tc k1 cTB *** k4 Tc k3 cTB k9 Tc k3 cTB k4, T (c k1 cTB k1 T) twice, c k1 cTB ***
work *** — *** 4 times in all, k4 Tc k3 cTB k9 Tc k3 cTB k4, Tc k1 cTB k1 Tc

10 Knit 240

11 K2 c s2kp c k3 cTB *** k3 cTB c s2kp c Tc k9 cTB c s2kp c Tc k3, Tc (k3 c s2kp c) twice, k3 cTB ***
work *** — *** 4 times in all, k3 cTB c s2kp c Tc k9 cTB c s2kp c Tc k3, Tc k3 c s2kp c k1

12 Knit 240

13 K1 Tc k1 cTB k1 Tc,
*** k2 Tc k1 cTB k1 Tc k1 cTB, k5, Tc k1 cTB k1 Tc k1 cTB k2 (cTB k1 Tc k1) twice, cTB k1 Tc ***
work *** — *** 4 times in all, k2 Tc k1 cTB k1 Tc k1 cTB, k5, Tc k1 cTB k1 Tc k1 cTB k2, cTB k1 Tc k1 cTB

14 **Knit 239 sts. ONLY** --- the last stitch is required for the s2kp at start of next row.

15 S2kp c k3 c s2kp c k1,
*** k2 cTB cTB k3 Tc Tc, k5, cTB cTB k3 Tc Tc k2, k1 (c s2kp c k3) twice, c s2kp c k1 ***
work *** — *** 4 times in all, k2 cTB cTB k3 Tc Tc, k5, cTB cTB k3 Tc Tc k2, k1 c s2kp c k3 c

16 K9 *** k3 cTB cTB k1 Tc Tc, k7, cTB cTB k1 Tc Tc k3, k17 ***
work *** — *** 4 times in all, k3 cTB cTB k1 Tc Tc, k7, cTB cTB k1 Tc Tc k3, k8

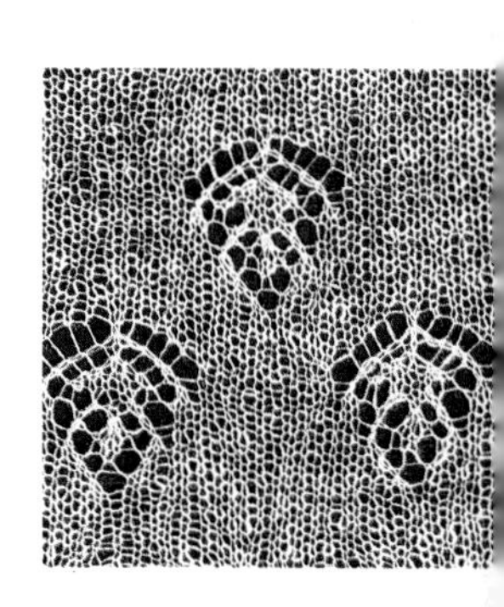

**ROW**

17 K1 cTB k1 Tc k1 cTB,
*** k4 cTB c s2kp c Tc, k9, cTB c s2kp c Tc k4, T (c k1 cTB k1 T) twice, c k1 cTB ***
work *** — *** 4 times in all, k4 cTB c s2kp c Tc k9, cTB c s2kp c Tc k4, Tc k1 cTB k1 Tc

18 K9 *** k5 cTB k1 Tc, k11, cTB k1 Tc k5, k17 ***
work *** — *** 4 times in all, k5 cTB k1 Tc, k11, cTB k1 Tc k5, k8

19 K2 c s2kp c k3 cTB *** k5 c s2kp c, k13, c s2kp c k5, Tc (k3 c s2kp c) twice, k3 cTB ***
work *** — *** 4 times in all, k5 c s2kp c, k13, c s2kp c k5, Tc k3 c s2kp c k1

20 Knit 240

This completes THE TWO-FERN SEQUENCE

21 K1 Tc k1 cTB k1 Tc *** k31 (cTB k1 Tc k1) twice, cTB k1 Tc ***
work *** — *** 4 times in all, k31, cTB k1 Tc k1 cTB

22 Knit **239 sts. ONLY** --- the last stitch is required for the s2kp at start of next row.

Continue with :
**MINIATURE LEAF & SINGLE FERN SEQUENCE**

23 S2kp c k3 c s2kp c k1 *** k8, k7 c skp k6, k8, k1 (c s2kp c k3) twice, c s2kp c k1 ***
work *** — *** 4 times in all, k8, k7 c skp k6, k8, k1 c s2kp c k3 c

24 Knit 240

25 K1 cTB k1 Tc k1 cTB *** k8, k5 Tc k1 cTB k5, k8, T (c k1 cTB k1 T) twice, c k1 cTB ***
work *** — *** 4 times in all, k8, k5 Tc k1 cTB k5, k8 Tc k1 cTB k1 Tc

26 Knit 240

27 K2 c s2kp c k3 cTB *** k7, k4 Tc k3 cTB k4, k7, Tc (k3 c s2kp c) twice, k3 cTB ***
work *** — *** 4 times in all, k7, k4 Tc k3 cTB k4, k7, Tc k3 c s2kp c k1

28 Knit 240

29 (K1 Tc k1 cTB) twice *** k9 cTB c s2kp c Tc k9 (Tc k1 cTB k1) 3 times, Tc k1 cTB ***
work *** — *** 4 times in all, k9 cTB c s2kp c Tc k9 Tc k1 cTB k1 Tc k1 cTB

30 Knit **239 sts. ONLY** --- the last stitch is required for the s2kp at start of next row.

31 (S2kp c k3 c) twice, TB *** k6 Tc k1 cTB k1 Tc k1 cTB k6 Tc (k3 c s2kp c) 3 times, k3 cTB ***
work *** — *** 4 times in all, k6 Tc k1 cTB k1 Tc k1 cTB k6, Tc k3 c s2kp c k3 c

32 Knit 240

**ROW**

33 (K1 cTB k1 Tc) twice, k1 *** k6 cTB cTB k3 Tc Tc k6, k1 c (TB k1 Tc k1 c) 3 times, TB k1 Tc k1 *** work *** — *** 4 times in all, k6, cTB cTB k3 Tc Tc k6, (k1 cTB k1 Tc) twice.

34 K13 *** k7 cTB cTB k1 Tc Tc k7, k25 *** , work *** — *** 4 times in all, k7 cTB cTB k1 Tc Tc k7, k12

35 K2 c s2kp c k3 c s2kp c k2 *** k8, cTB c s2kp c Tc k8, k2 c (s2kp c k3 c) 3 times, s2kp c k2 *** work *** — *** 4 times in all, k8, cTB c s2kp c Tc k8, k2 c s2kp c k3 c s2kp c k1

36 K13 *** k9 cTB k1 Tc k9, k25 *** , work *** — *** 4 times in all, k9 cTB k1 Tc k9, k12

37 (K1 Tc k1 cTB) twice, k1 *** k10, c s2kp c k10, k1 T (c k1 c TB k1 T) 3 times, c k1 c TB k1 *** work *** — *** 4 times in all, k10, c s2kp c k10, (k1 Tc k1 cTB) twice

38 Knit **239 sts. ONLY** --- the last stitch is required for the s2kp at start of next row.

This completes THE SINGLE FERN SEQUENCE

39 (S2kp c k3 c) twice, TB *** k23 Tc (k3 c s2kp c) 3 times, k3 cTB *** work *** — *** 4 times in all, k23, Tc k3 c s2kp c k3 c

40 Knit 240

41 (K1 cTB k1 Tc) repeat to end of row.

42 Knit 240

43 K2 c s2kp c (k3 c s2kp c) repeat ( — ) to last st., k1

44 Knit 240

45 (K1 Tc k1 cTB) repeat to end of row.

46 Knit **239 sts. ONLY**
--- the last stitch is required for the s2kp at start of next row.

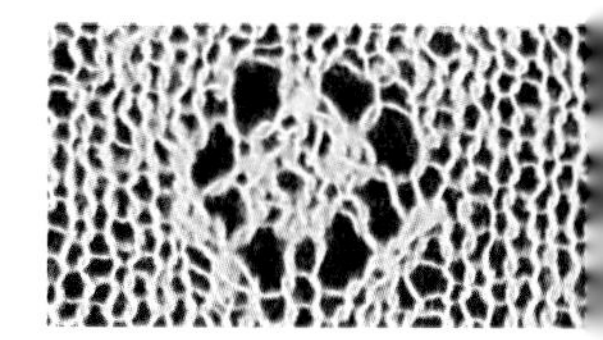

47 (S2kp c k3 c) repeat to end of row.

48 Knit 240

49 Knit 240

**DIVIDE FOR BACK OPENING & ARMHOLES**

**NOTE** : All stitch counts **INCLUDE** stitch remaining on needle after casting off.

Knit 57 (left back) cast off 6 sts., knit 114 (front) cast off 6 sts., knit 57 (right back)
Next row — cast on 5 sts. for back fastening, knit these 5 sts. plus 57 for **LEFT BACK, TURN,**
Cast off 2 sts., purl 55, knit 5
Next row — knit 5, k53 T (5 + 54 sts.)
Break off wool.

**FRONT** : With right side of work facing, rejoin wool at LEFT armhole,
Cast off 2 sts., knit 112, **TURN,** cast off 2 sts. purlwise, purl 110
Next row — TB k106 T (108 sts.)
Break off wool.

**RIGHT BACK** : With right side of work facing, rejoin wool at RIGHT armhole,
Cast off 2 sts., knit 55, **TURN,** cast on 5 sts. for back fastening, knit these 5 sts., purl 55
Next row — T k53, k5 (54 + 5 sts.)
Break off wool

**NOTE** : At this point it is recommended that stitches be threaded on to a light-coloured wool, leaving extra length, and the garment should be dressed as per instructions.
After dressing, replace stitches on needle.

**FRONT** : With wrong side of work facing, rejoin wool at RIGHT-HAND SIDE and proceed as follows :
(PT purl 19) 5 times, purl 1, PT (102 sts.)
Decrease for yoke — K3 (T k1) to last 3 sts., k3 (70 sts.)
Next row — purl

Continue, working the 4 rows of the Bird's Eye stitch sequence, 5 times, (20 rows).

**BIRD'S EYE STITCH SEQUENCE**

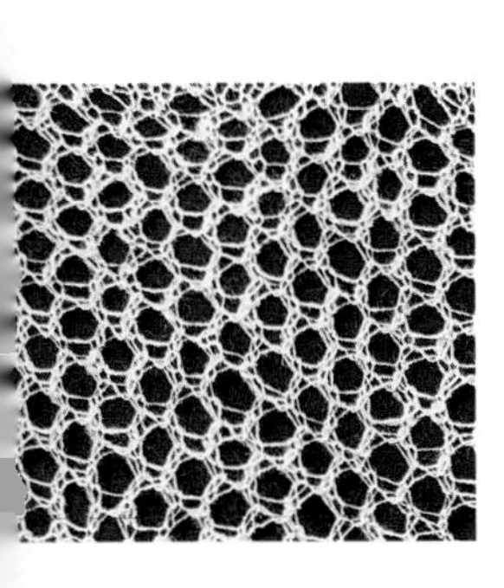

**ROW**

1 K1 (T c T) repeat ( — ) to last st., k1

2 K2 (k1 and p1 into made stitch, k2) repeat ( — ) to end of row

3 K3 (T c T) repeat ( — ) to last 3 sts., k3

4 K3 (k1, k1 and p1 into made stitch, k1) repeat ( — ) to last 3 sts., k3

**NOTE** : The number of stitches in rows will fluctuate — Rows 1 + 3 will reduce the number of stitches,
Rows 2 + 4 will increase the number of stitches.

FRONT NECK SHAPING : With right side of work facing proceed as follows :

| **ROW** | | |
|---|---|---|
| 1 | K1 (T c T) 17 times, k1 | (53) |
| 2 | K2 (k1 and p1 into made stitch, k2) 9 times, k1 and p1 into made stitch, **TURN** | (40) |
| 3 | K10 — leave these on pin for front neck, and continue....cast off 2 sts. (T c T) 6 times, k3 | (22) |
| 4 | K3 (k1, k1 and p1 into made stitch, k1) 6 times, k1 | (28) |
| 5 | Cast off 2 sts. (T c T) 6 times, k1 | (20) |
| 6 | K2 (k1 and p1 into made stitch, k2) 6 times | (26) |
| 7 | Cast off 2 sts. (T c T) 5 times, k3 | (19) |
| 8 | K3 (k1, k1 and p1 into made stitch, k1) 5 times, k1 | (24) |
| 9 | T, k1 (T c T) 5 times, k1 | (18) |
| 10 | K2 (k1 and p1 into made stitch, k2) 4 times, k1 and p1 into made st., s2kp | (21) |

Leave these 21 stitches on pin and rejoin wool at neck edge of LEFT FRONT and proceed as follows :

| | | |
|---|---|---|
| Work 2nd pattern row — | K2 (k1 and p1 into made stitch, k2) 7 times | (30) |
| 3 | K3 (T c T) 6 times, k3 | (24) |
| 4 | Cast off 2 sts. k1 (k1 and p1 into made stitch, k2) 6 times, k2 | (28) |
| 5 | K1 (T c T) 6 times, T k1 | (21) |
| 6 | Cast off 2 sts. (k1 and p1 into made stitch, k2) 6times | (25) |
| 7 | K3 (T c T) 5 times, k2 | (20) |
| 8 | Cast off 2 sts. (k1 and p1 into made stitch, k2) 5 times, k2 | (23) |
| 9 | K1 (T c T) 5 times, k2 | (18) |
| 10 | S2kp (k1 and p1 into made stitch, k2) 5 times | (21) |

Leave these 21 stitches on pin

**LEFT BACK** : With wrong side of work facing, rejoin wool at armhole edge and proceed as follows :
(Purl 12 PT) 3 times, purl 12, k5 (51 + 5 sts.)
Decrease for yoke — K5 (T k1) 17 times (5 garter + 34 sts.)
Next row — Purl 34, k5

Continue, working the 4 rows of the Bird's Eye stitch sequence, 5 times, (20 rows), keeping the 5 garter stitches at centre back.

**BIRD'S EYE STITCH SEQUENCE**

**ROW**

1 K1 (T c T) repeat ( — ) to last st., k1

2 K2 (k1 and p1 into made stitch, k2) repeat ( — ) to end of row

3 K3 (T c T) repeat ( — ) to last 3 sts., k3

4 K3 (k1, k1 and p1 into made stitch, k1) repeat ( — ) to last 3 sts., k3

LEFT BACK NECK SHAPING : With right side of work facing, proceed as follows :

| | | |
|---|---|---|
| 1 | K5 garter sts. + 5 sts. (hold on pin), cast off 2 sts., k1 (T c T) 6 times, k1 | (21) |
| 2 | K2 (k1 and p1 into made stitch, k2) 6 times, k1 | (27) |
| 3 | Cast off 3 sts. (T c T) 5 times, k3 | (19) |
| 4 | K3 (k1, k1 and p1 into made stitch, k1) 5 times, k1 | (24) |
| 5 | Cast off 2 sts. (T c T) 5 times, k1 | (17) |
| 6 | K2 (k1 and p1 into made stitch, k2) 5 times | (22) |
| 7 | T k1 (T c T) 4 times, k3 | (17) |
| 8 | K3 (k1, k1 and p1 into made stitch, k1) 4 times, k2 | (21) |

Leave these 21 stitches on pin.

**RIGHT BACK** : With wrong side of work facing, rejoin wool at back opening (garter st. edge) of RIGHT BACK and proceed as follows :
Knit 5 (purl 12, PT) 3 times, purl 12 (5 + 51 sts.)
Decrease for yoke — (T k1) 17 times, k5 (34 + 5 garter sts.)
Next row — K5, purl 34

Continue, working the 4 rows of the Bird's Eye stitch sequence, 5 times, (20 rows), keeping the 5 garter stitches at centre back.

**BIRD'S EYE STITCH SEQUENCE**

**ROW**

1 K1 (T c T) repeat ( — ) to last st., k1

2 K2 (k1 and p1 into made stitch, k2) repeat ( — ) to end of row

3 K3 (T c T) repeat ( — ) to last 3 sts., k3

4 K3 (k1, k1 and p1 into made stitch, k1) repeat ( — ) to last 3 sts., k3

RIGHT BACK NECK SHAPING : With right side of work facing, proceed as follows :

| | | |
|---|---|---|
| 1 | K1 (T c T) 6 times, k4 — leaving 5 sts. + 5 garter sts. (hold on pin) | (23) |
| 2 | Cast off 2 sts., k2 (k1 and p1 into made stitch, k2) 6 times | (27) |
| 3 | K3 (T c T) 5 times, k4 | (22) |
| 4 | Cast off 3 sts. k1 (k1 and p1 into made stitch, k2) 5 times, k2 | (24) |
| 5 | K1 (T c T) 5 times, k3 | (19) |
| 6 | Cast off 2 sts. k1 (k1 and p1 into made stitch, k2) 5 times | (22) |
| 7 | K3 (T c T) 4 times, k3 | (18) |
| 8 | T k2 (k1 and p1 into made stitch, k2) 4 times, k2 | (21) |

Leave these 21 stitches on pin.

Graft together shoulder seams and proceed with neckband :

**NECKBAND** :
With No.12 needle and right side of work facing, rejoin wool and knit up 10 stitches from LEFT BACK, 30 from LEFT SIDE NECK, 10 from CENTRE FRONT, 30 from RIGHT SIDE NECK and 5 of the remaining 10 stitches at RIGHT BACK (85 stitches).
The 5 garter stitches at CENTRE BACK EDGE will turn under at RIGHT BACK and the stitches will be purled together with the first 5 stitches of the next row. Work a further 8 rows in stocking stitch.

Cast off loosely. Turn to inside and stitch down. RIGHT side of back opening will finish on top of 5 garter stitches from LEFT back. Stitch in place and sew on press fasteners at even intervals.

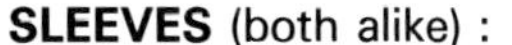

**SLEEVES** (both alike) :
With No.11 needle, cast on 10 stitches loosely
Knit one row
Starter rows — Slip 1 purlwise, Tc T k5 (9)
Slip 1 purlwise, knit to end (9)

**FOUR HOLE BORDER LACE**

**ROW**

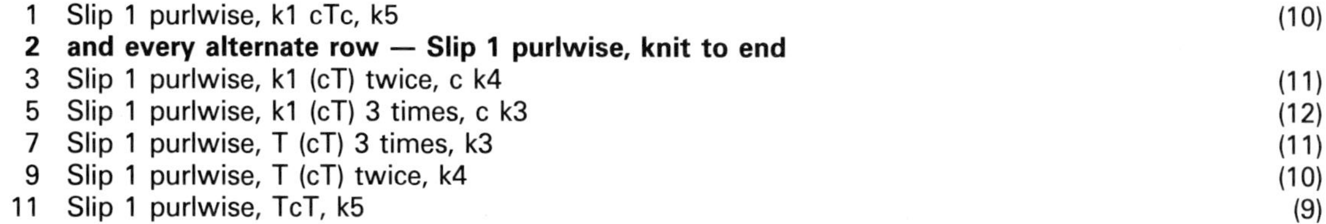

1 Slip 1 purlwise, k1 cTc, k5 (10)
**2 and every alternate row — Slip 1 purlwise, knit to end**
3 Slip 1 purlwise, k1 (cT) twice, c k4 (11)
5 Slip 1 purlwise, k1 (cT) 3 times, c k3 (12)
7 Slip 1 purlwise, T (cT) 3 times, k3 (11)
9 Slip 1 purlwise, T (cT) twice, k4 (10)
11 Slip 1 purlwise, TcT, k5 (9)
12 Slip 1 purlwise, knit to end

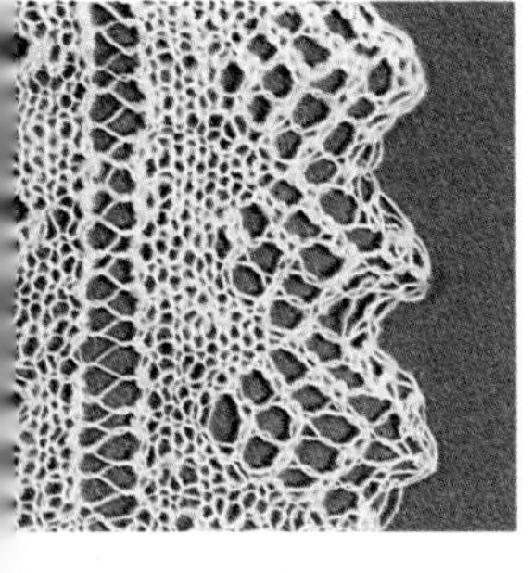

**These 12 rows form one scallop,** and are worked continuously until 10 scallops have been completed.
Cast off loosely.
With right side of work facing, pick up 61 sts. along straight edge of border lace and starting at RIGHT-HAND side, knit one row through back loops
Next row — (decrease) purl 2, (PT) 28 times, purl 3 (33)
Next row — (increase) knit 2, knit twice into next 29 stitches, k1 (61)
Purl one row
Knit one row

**NOTE** : At this point the work will be transposed so that the cuff may be turned right side out.

Continue, working the 8 rows of the Miniature Leaf stitch sequence, 6 times, (48 rows).

**MINIATURE LEAF STITCH SEQUENCE**

**ROW**

1 K1 (Tc k1 c TB k1) 10 times
**2 and every alternate row — purl**
3 TB (c k3 c s2kp) 9 times, c k3 cT
5 K1 (cTB k1 Tc k1) 10 times
7 K2 (c s2kp c k3) 9 times, c s2kp c k2
8 Purl (61)

**ARMHOLE DECREASE,** (keeping pattern in sequence) :

Cast off 3 sts., at the beginning of the next 2 rows, then,
Cast off 2 sts., at the beginning of the next 4 rows, then,
Cast off 1 st., at the beginning of the next 4 rows. (43 sts.)

Continue, working in pattern for a further 30 rows.

**SHAPE TOP OF SLEEVE :**

Cast off 3 sts., at the beginning of the next 2 rows, then,
Cast off 5 sts., at the beginning of the next 2 rows, then,
Cast off 7 sts., at the beginning of the next 2 rows. (13 sts.)

Next row — Work in pattern

Next row — Cast off remaining stitches purlwise.

**TO DRESS ROBE :** Wash main part of garment and sleeves separately **BY HAND ONLY** in lukewarm soapy water, squeezing gently. Rinse in lukewarm water. Roll up in a towel to absorb excess moisture. Stretch out, away from heat or sun and dry flat, shaping garment and pinning out points of border lace. Decorate with ribbon if required.

**DRESS SLEEVES :** Dress sleeves and lay flat, pinned out to shape, also pinning points of border lace. Sew up sleeve seams, matching pattern, gather tops and fit into armhole. Turn up border lace cuffs and lightly stitch at seam. Thread narrow ribbon through holes and tie on outside of cuffs.

# *Fine Lace Stole and Scarf*

## KNITTED IN 1-PLY COBWEB WOOL

**STOLE Size — 60" x 22" (152cm x 56cm)**
**SCARF Size — 45" x 15" (114cm x 38cm)**

**MATERIALS** : For **STOLE** — 5 hanks of cobweb lace Shetland wool
or for **SCARF** — 3 hanks of cobweb lace Shetland wool
1 circular needle — size 11 (3mm) — 24" (60cm) long
or 1 pair of needles — size 11 (3mm)

This pattern is offered as a stole or scarf — instructions are in full for both garments. These can be knitted on two needles, but the circular needle is recommended to accommodate the stitches more easily. The garments are worked from Ring stitch border, through the Print of the Wave centre and completed with another Ring stitch border.
Particular care should be taken to work at a fairly slack tension at all times. For your guidance the pattern shows the edging lace separated from the main part of the work by a row of dots.

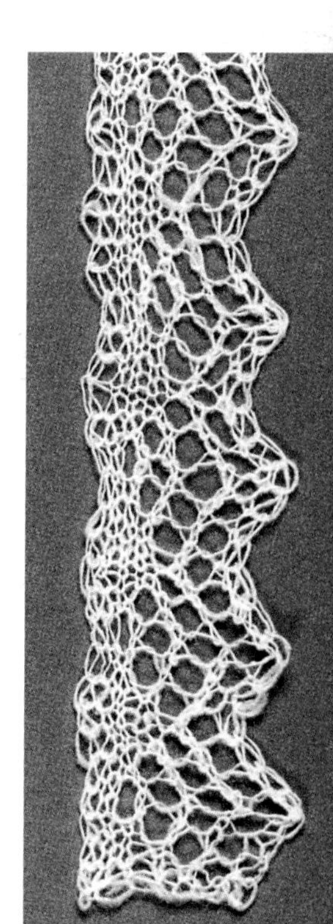

## STOLE — KNITTING INSTRUCTIONS

**NOTE** : Throughout the whole work, the first stitch of each row is worked **slip 1 purlwise ( S1pw ).**

Cast on 9 sts. **VERY** loosely, and knit the following 12 rows.

1st Row : S1pw k1 cTc, k5 (10)

**2nd and every alternate row : S1pw knit to end**

3rd Row : S1pw k1 (cT) twice, c k4 (11)

5th Row : S1pw k1 (cT) 3 times, c k3 (12)

7th Row : S1pw T (cT) 3 times, k3 (11)

9th Row : S1pw T (cT) twice, k4 (10)

11th Row : S1pw TcT, k5 (9)

12th Row : S1pw knit to end.

**These 12 rows form one scallop of edging lace,** and are worked continuously until 21 scallops have been completed.

# *Fine Lace Stole & Scarf*

With wrong side of work facing, pick up 10 sts. from the cast-on edge plus 126 sts. from straight edge of edging lace and take up 9 sts. from the last scallop. Continue with the corner turning sequence and twelve 'starter' rows as follows : —

**ROW**

1 + 2 S1pw k1 cTc k5, **TURN,** k10 (to outside edge), and continue S1pw k1 (cT) twice, c k4....knit 126....k10

3 + 4 S1pw k1 (cT) twice, c k4, **TURN,** k11, and continue S1pw k1 (cT) 3 times, c k3....purl 62, purl into back and front of next stitch, purl further 63 sts....k11 (edges plus 127 sts.)

5 + 6 S1pw k1 (cT) 3 times, c k3, **TURN,** k12, and continue S1pw T (cT) 3 times, k3....knit 127....k12

7 + 8 S1pw T (cT) 3 times, k3, **TURN,** k11, and continue S1pw T (cT) twice, k4....purl 127....k11

9 + 10 S1pw T (cT) twice, k4, **TURN,** k10, and continue S1pw TcT k5....(k1 cTc 3T c) 21 times, k1....k10

11 + 12 S1pw TcT k5, **TURN,** k9, and continue S1pw k1 cTc k5....k1 (cT k1 Tc k1) 21 times....k9

**This completes the corner turning sequence.**

**RING STITCH & EDGING LACE SEQUENCE**

13 S1pw k1 cTc k5....k2 c 3T (c k3 c 3T) 20 times, c k2....k10

14 S1pw k1 (cT) twice, c k4....k1 (Tc k1 cT k1) 21 times....k10

15 S1pw k1 (cT) twice, c k4....(c 3T c k1 cT) 21 times, cT....k10
**NOTE** : The last 'T' of rows 15, 23 and 31, takes up the first stitch of the edging lace.

16 S1pw k1 (cT) 3 times, c k3....k1 (Tc k1 cT k1) 21 times....k11

17 S1pw k1 (cT) 3 times, c k3....Tc k3 c (3T c k3 c) 20 times, T....k12

18 S1pw T (cT) 3 times, k3....k1 (cT k1 Tc k1) 21 times....k12

19 S1pw T (cT) 3 times, k3....(k1 cTc 3T c) 21 times, k1....k11

20 S1pw T (cT) twice, k4....k1 (cT k1 Tc k1) 21 times....k11

21 S1pw T (cT) twice, k4....k2 c 3T (c k3 c 3T) 20 times, c k2....k10

22 S1pw TcT k5....k1 (Tc k1 cT k1) 21 times....k10

23 S1pw TcT k5....(c 3T c k1 cT) 21 times, cT....k8

24 S1pw k1 cTc k5....k1 (Tc k1 cT k1) 21 times....k9

25 S1pw k1 cTc k5....Tc k3 c (3T c k3 c) 20 times, T....k10

26 S1pw k1 (cT) twice, c k4....k1 (cT k1 Tc k1) 21 times....k10

27 S1pw k1 (cT) twice, c k4....(k1 cTc 3T c) 21 times, k1....k11

28 S1pw k1 (cT) 3 times, c k3....k1 (cT k1 Tc k1) 21 times....k11

29 S1pw k1 (cT) 3 times, c k3....k2 c 3T (c k3 c 3T) 20 times, c k2....k12

30 S1pw T (cT) 3 times, k3....k1 (Tc k1 cT k1) 21 times....k12

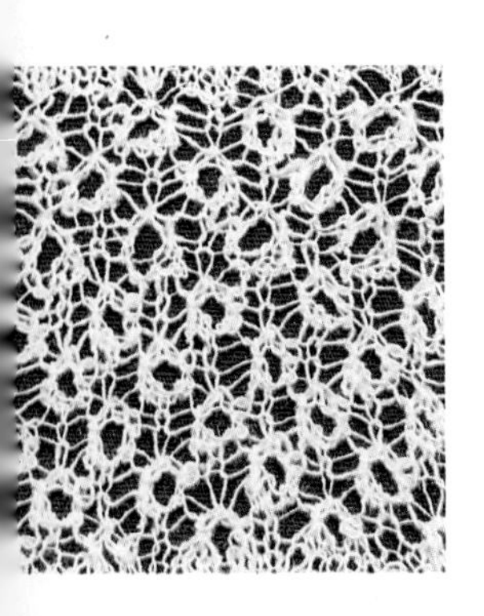

**ROW**

31 S1pw T (cT) 3 times, k3....(c 3T c k1 cT) 21 times, cT....k10

32 S1pw T (cT) twice, k4....k1 (Tc k1 cT k1) 21 times....k11

33 S1pw T (cT) twice, k4....Tc k3 c (3T c k3 c) 20 times, T....k10

34 S1pw TcT k5....k1 (cT k1 Tc k1) 21 times....k10

35 S1pw TcT k5....(k1 cTc 3T c) 21 times, k1....k9

36 S1pw k1 cTc k5....k1 (cT k1 Tc k1) 21 times....k9

37 S1pw k1 cTc k5....k2 c 3T (c k3 c 3T) 20 times, c k2....k10

38 S1pw k1 (cT) twice, c k4....k1 (Tc k1 cT k1) 21 times....k10

39 S1pw k1 (cT) twice, c k4....(c 3T c k1 cT) 21 times, cT....k10

**NOTE** : The last 'T' of rows 39, 47 and 55, takes up the first stitch of the edging lace.

40 S1pw k1 (cT) 3 times, c k3....k1 (Tc k1 cT k1) 21 times....k11

41 S1pw k1 (cT) 3 times, c k3....Tc k3 c (3T c k3 c) 20 times, T....k12

42 S1pw T (cT) 3 times, k3....k1 (cT k1 Tc k1) 21 times....k12

43 S1pw T (cT) 3 times, k3....(k1 cTc 3T c) 21 times, k1....k11

44 S1pw T (cT) twice, k4....k1 (cT k1 Tc k1) 21 times....k11

45 S1pw T (cT) twice, k4....k2 c 3T (c k3 c 3T) 20 times, c k2....k10

46 S1pw TcT k5....k1 (Tc k1 cT k1) 21 times....k10

47 S1pw TcT k5....(c 3T c k1 cT) 21 times, cT....k8

48 S1pw k1 cTc k5....k1 (Tc k1 cT k1) 21 times....k9

49 S1pw k1 cTc k5....Tc k3 c (3T c k3 c) 20 times, T....k10

50 S1pw k1 (cT) twice, c k4....k1 (cT k1 Tc k1) 21 times....k10

51 S1pw k1 (cT) twice, c k4....(k1 cTc 3T c) 21 times, k1....k11

52 S1pw k1 (cT) 3 times, c k3....k1 (cT k1 Tc k1) 21 times....k11

53 S1pw k1 (cT) 3 times, c k3....k2 c 3T (c k3 c 3T) 20 times, c k2....k12

54 S1pw T (cT) 3 times, k3....k1 (Tc k1 cT k1) 21 times....k12

55 S1pw T (cT) 3 times, k3....(c 3T c k1 cT) 21 times, cT....k10

56 S1pw T (cT) twice, k4....k1 (Tc k1 cT k1) 21 times....k11

57 S1pw T (cT) twice, k4....Tc k3 c (3T c k3 c) 20 times, T....k10

58 S1pw TcT k5....k1 (cT k1 Tc k1) 21 times....k10

**Work as Rows 35 to 58 a further three times.**

This completes the RING STITCH & EDGING LACE SEQUENCE of 15 patterns and 10 scallops.

**BREAK ROWS & EDGING LACE SEQUENCE**

**ROW**

131 S1pw TcT k5....knit 127....k9

132 S1pw k1 cTc k5....purl 127....k9

133 S1pw k1 cTc k5....knit 127....k10

134 S1pw k1 (cT) twice, c k4....**KNIT 127**....k10

135 S1pw k1 (cT) twice, c k4....(cT) 64 times....k10

136 S1pw k1 (cT) 3 times, c k3....(cT) 64 times....k10

137 S1pw k1 (cT) 3 times, c k3....(cT) 64 times....k11

138 S1pw T (cT) 3 times, k3....**KNIT 127**....k12

139 S1pw T (cT) 3 times, k3....knit 127....k11

140 S1pw T (cT) twice, k4....purl 127....k11

141 S1pw T (cT) twice, k4....knit 127....k10

142 S1pw TcT k5....purl 127....k10

**PRINT of the WAVE & EDGING LACE SEQUENCE** (centre)

143 S1pw TcT k5....k1 cT k1, Tc Tc Tc (k1 T k3 T k1, c k1 c, Tc Tc) 8 times, k1, k2 cT....k9

144 S1pw k1 cTc k5....k1 cT k1, purl 119, k2 cT....k9

145 S1pw k1 cTc k5....k1 cT k1, Tc Tc Tc (k1 T k1 T k1, c k3 c, Tc Tc) 8 times, k1, k2 cT....k10

146 S1pw k1 (cT) twice, c k4....k1 cT k1, purl 119, k2 cT....k10

147 S1pw k1 (cT) twice, c k4....k1 cT k1, Tc Tc Tc (k1 s2kp k1, c k5 c, Tc Tc) 8 times, k1, k2 cT....k11

148 S1pw k1 (cT) 3 times, c k3....k1 cT k1, purl 119, k2 cT....k11

149 S1pw k1 (cT) 3 times, c k3....k1 cT k1, k1 cT cT (c k1 c, k1 T k3 T k1, cT cT) 8 times, cT k2 cT....k12

150 S1pw T (cT) 3 times, k3....k1 cT k1, purl 119, k2 cT....k12

151 S1pw T (cT) 3 times, k3....k1 cT k1, k1 cT cT (c k3 c, k1 T k1 T k1, cT cT) 8 times, cT k2 cT....k11

152 S1pw T (cT) twice, k4....k1 cT k1, purl 119, k2 cT....k11

153 S1pw T (cT) twice, k4....k1 cT k1, k1 cT cT (c k5 c, k1 s2kp k1, cT cT) 8 times, cT k2 cT....k10

154 S1pw TcT k5....k1 cT k1, purl 119, k2 cT....k10

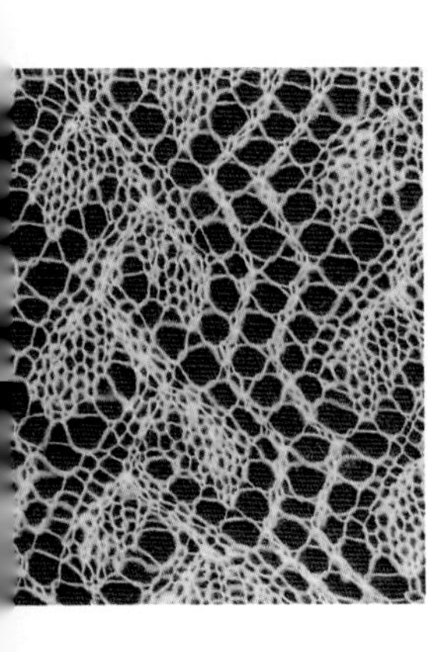

**Work as Rows 143 to 154 a further twenty-three times,** giving 24 patterns.

**Row 431,** continue with the **BREAK ROWS & EDGING LACE, working as Rows 131 to 142 ONCE only.**

**Row 443,** continue with the **RING STITCH & EDGING LACE, working as Rows 35 to 58, FOUR times,** giving 12 patterns of the RING STITCH and 8 scallops.

**ROW**

539 S1pw TcT k5....(k1 cTc 3T c) 21 times, k1....k9

540 S1pw k1 cTc k5....k1 (cT k1 Tc k1) 21 times....k9

541 S1pw k1 cTc k5....k2 c 3T (c k3 c 3T) 20 times, c k2....k10

542 S1pw k1 (cT) twice, c k4....k1 (Tc k1 cT k1) 21 times....k10

543 S1pw k1 (cT) twice, c k4....(c 3T c k1 cT) 21 times, cT....k10
**NOTE** : The last 'T' of rows 543, 551 and 560, takes up the first stitch of the edging lace.

544 S1pw k1 (cT) 3 times, c k3....k1 (Tc k1 cT k1) 21 times....k11

545 S1pw k1 (cT) 3 times, c k3....Tc k3 c (3T c k3 c) 20 times, T....k12

546 S1pw T (cT) 3 times, k3....k1 (cT k1 Tc k1) 21 times....k12

547 S1pw T (cT) 3 times, k3....(k1 cTc 3T c) 21 times, k1....k11

548 S1pw T (cT) twice, k4....k1 (cT k1 Tc k1) 21 times....k11

549 S1pw T (cT) twice, k4....k2 c 3T (c k3 c 3T) 20 times, c k2....k10

550 S1pw TcT k5....k1 (Tc k1 cT k1) 21 times....k10

551 S1pw TcT k5....(c 3T c k1 cT) 21 times, cT....k8

552 S1pw k1 cTc k5....k1 (Tc k1 cT k1) 21 times....k9

553 S1pw k1 cTc k5....Tc k3 c (3T c k3 c) 20 times, T....k10

554 S1pw k1 (cT) twice, c k4....k1 (cT k1 Tc k1) 21 times....k10

555 S1pw k1 (cT) twice, c k4....(k1 cTc 3T c) 21 times, k1....k11

556 S1pw k1 (cT) 3 times, c k3....k1 (cT k1 Tc k1) 21 times....k11

557 S1pw k1 (cT) 3 times, c k3....k2 c 3T (c k3 c 3T) 20 times, c k2....k12

558 S1pw T (cT) 3 times, k3....k1 (Tc k1 cT k1) 21 times....k12

**Continue with corner turning as follows : —**

559 + 560 S1pw T (cT) 3 times, k3, **TURN,** k11, and continue S1pw T (cT) twice, k4....(c 3T c k1 cT) 21 times, cT....k10

561 + 562 S1pw T (cT) twice, k4, **TURN,** k10, and continue S1pw TcT k5....k1 (Tc k1 cT k1) 21 times....k10

563 + 564 S1pw TcT k5, **TURN,** k9, and continue S1pw k1 cTc k5....Tc k3 c (3T c k3 c) 20 times, T....k9

565 + 566 S1pw k1 cTc k5, **TURN,** k10, and continue S1pw k1 (cT) twice, c k4....k1 (cT k1 Tc k1) 21 times....k10

This completes the RING STITCH & EDGING LACE SEQUENCE.

Work the following six rows to complete the main body of the garment.

**ROW**

567 + 568 S1pw k1 (cT) twice, c k4, **TURN,** k11, and continue S1pw k1 (cT) 3 times, c k3....knit 127....k11

569 + 570 S1pw k1 (cT) 3 times, c k3, **TURN,** k12, and continue S1pw T (cT) 3 times, k3....purl 127....k12

571 + 572 S1pw T (cT) 3 times, k3, **TURN,** k11, and continue S1pw T (cT) twice, k4....knit 127....k11

With wrong side of work facing, continue working on edging lace ONLY from the 9th row (below).

Leave 127 stitches plus the 10 remaining edging stitches on a spare needle.

9th Row : S1pw T (cT) twice, k4 (10)

10th Row : S1pw knit to end.

11th Row : S1pw TcT, k5 (9)

12th Row : S1pw knit to end.

Continue with the edging lace sequence of 12 rows.

1st Row : S1pw k1 cTc, k5 (10)

**2nd and every alternate row : S1pw knit to end**

3rd Row : S1pw k1 (cT) twice, c k4 (11)

5th Row : S1pw k1 (cT) 3 times, c k3 (12)

7th Row : S1pw T (cT) 3 times, k3 (11)

9th Row : S1pw T (cT) twice, k4 (10)

11th Row : S1pw TcT, k5 (9)

12th Row : S1pw knit to end.

Work continuously until 21 scallops have been completed.

Pick up the 127 sts. from the straight edge and graft together with those on the spare needle and continue grafting edging stitches to complete.

**TO DRESS THE GARMENT** : Wash **BY HAND ONLY** in lukewarm soapy water, squeezing gently. Rinse in lukewarm water. Roll up in a towel to absorb excess moisture. Stretch out to the approximate size 60" x 22" away from heat or sun, on a frame or pin out main garment and each scallop point on a white sheet and dry flat.

# *Fine Lace Scarf*

**KNITTED IN 1-PLY COBWEB WOOL**

**Size — 45'' x 15'' (114cm x 38cm)**

**MATERIALS** : 3 hanks of cobweb lace Shetland wool
1 circular needle — size 11 (3mm) — 24" (60cm) long
or 1 pair of needles — size 11 (3mm)

The following is the detailed pattern for the scarf as a smaller version of the stole pattern (page 27). If the knitter wishes to vary the centre panel by using a different stitch, the 12-row sequence on page 39 may be substituted for rows 143-154 (page 36) without alteration to the remainder of the pattern.

## SCARF — KNITTING INSTRUCTIONS

**NOTE : Throughout the whole work, the first stitch of each row is worked slip 1 purlwise ( S1pw ).**

Cast on 9 sts. **VERY** loosely, and knit the following 12 rows.

1st Row : S1pw k1 cTc, k5 (10)

**2nd and every alternate row : S1pw knit to end**

3rd Row : S1pw k1 (cT) twice, c k4 (11)

5th Row : S1pw k1 (cT) 3 times, c k3 (12)

7th Row : S1pw T (cT) 3 times, k3 (11)

9th Row : S1pw T (cT) twice, k4 (10)

11th Row : S1pw TcT, k5 (9)

12th Row : S1pw knit to end.

**These 12 rows form one scallop of edging lace,** and are worked continuously until 14 scallops have been completed.

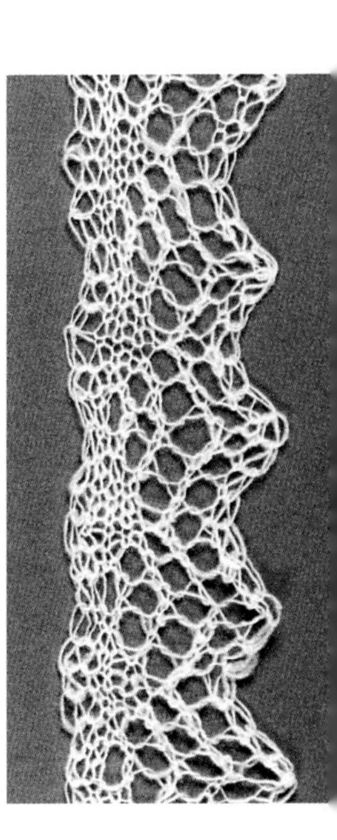

With wrong side of work facing, pick up 10 sts. from the cast-on edge plus 84 sts. from straight edge of edging lace and take up 9 sts. from the last scallop. Continue with the corner turning sequence and twelve 'starter' rows as follows : —

**ROW**

1 + 2 S1pw k1 cTc k5, **TURN,** k10 (to outside edge), and continue S1pw k1 (cT) twice, c k4....knit 84....k10

3 + 4 S1pw k1 (cT) twice, c k4, **TURN,** k11, and continue S1pw k1 (cT) 3 times, c k3....purl 41, purl into back and front of next stitch, purl further 42 sts....k11 (edges plus 85 sts.)

5 + 6 S1pw k1 (cT) 3 times, c k3, **TURN,** k12, and continue S1pw T (cT) 3 times, k3....knit 85....k12

7 + 8 S1pw T (cT) 3 times, k3, **TURN,** k11, and continue S1pw T (cT) twice, k4....purl 85....k11

9 + 10 S1pw T (cT) twice, k4, **TURN,** k10, and continue S1pw TcT k5....(k1 cTc 3T c) 14 times, k1....k10

11 + 12 S1pw TcT k5, **TURN,** k9, and continue S1pw k1 cTc k5....k1 (cT k1 Tc k1) 14 times....k9

**This completes the corner turning sequence.**

**RING STITCH & EDGING LACE SEQUENCE**

13 S1pw k1 cTc k5....k2 c 3T (c k3 c 3T) 13 times, c k2....k10

14 S1pw k1 (cT) twice, c k4....k1 (Tc k1 cT k1) 14 times....k10

15 S1pw k1 (cT) twice, c k4....(c 3T c k1 cT) 14 times, cT....k10

**NOTE** : The last 'T' of rows 15, 23 and 31, takes up the first stitch of the edging lace.

16 S1pw k1 (cT) 3 times, c k3....k1 (Tc k1 cT k1) 14 times....k11

17 S1pw k1 (cT) 3 times, c k3....Tc k3 c (3T c k3 c) 13 times, T....k12

18 S1pw T (cT) 3 times, k3....k1 (cT k1 Tc k1) 14 times....k12

19 S1pw T (cT) 3 times, k3....(k1 cTc 3T c) 14 times, k1....k11

20 S1pw T (cT) twice, k4....k1 (cT k1 Tc k1) 14 times....k11

21 S1pw T (cT) twice, k4....k2 c 3T (c k3 c 3T) 13 times, c k2....k10

22 S1pw TcT k5....k1 (Tc k1 cT k1) 14 times....k10

23 S1pw TcT k5....(c 3T c k1 cT) 14 times, cT....k8

24 S1pw k1 cTc k5....k1 (Tc k1 cT k1) 14 times....k9

25 S1pw k1 cTc k5....Tc k3 c (3T c k3 c) 13 times, T....k10

26 S1pw k1 (cT) twice, c k4....k1 (cT k1 Tc k1) 14 times....k10

27 S1pw k1 (cT) twice, c k4....(k1 cTc 3T c) 14 times, k1....k11

28 S1pw k1 (cT) 3 times, c k3....k1 (cT k1 Tc k1) 14 times....k11

29 S1pw k1 (cT) 3 times, c k3....k2 c 3T (c k3 c 3T) 13 times, c k2....k12

30 S1pw T (cT) 3 times, k3....k1 (Tc k1 cT k1) 14 times....k12

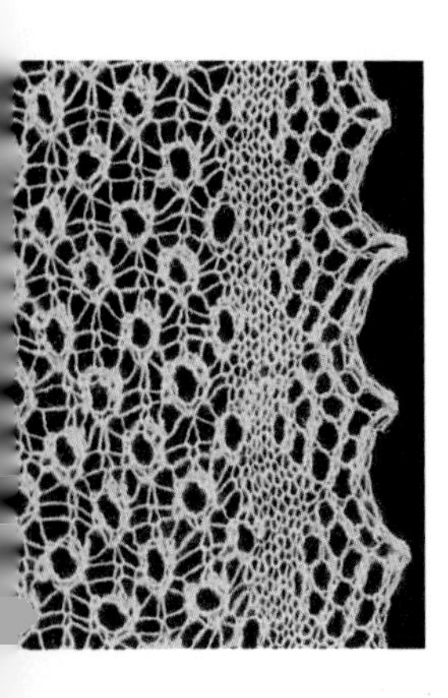

**ROW**

31 S1pw T (cT) 3 times, k3....(c 3T c k1 cT) 14 times, cT....k10
32 S1pw T (cT) twice, k4....k1 (Tc k1 cT k1) 14 times....k11
33 S1pw T (cT) twice, k4....Tc k3 c (3T c k3 c) 13 times, T....k10
34 S1pw TcT k5....k1 (cT k1 Tc k1) 14 times....k10

35 S1pw TcT k5....(k1 cTc 3T c) 14 times, k1....k9
36 S1pw k1 cTc k5....k1 (cT k1 Tc k1) 14 times....k9
37 S1pw k1 cTc k5....k2 c 3T (c k3 c 3T) 13 times, c k2....k10
38 S1pw k1 (cT) twice, c k4....k1 (Tc k1 cT k1) 14 times....k10
39 S1pw k1 (cT) twice, c k4....(c 3T c k1 cT) 14 times, cT....k10
**NOTE** : The last 'T' of rows 39, 47 and 55, takes up the first stitch of the edging lace.
40 S1pw k1 (cT) 3 times, c k3....k1 (Tc k1 cT k1) 14 times....k11
41 S1pw k1 (cT) 3 times, c k3....Tc k3 c (3T c k3 c) 13 times, T....k12
42 S1pw T (cT) 3 times, k3....k1 (cT k1 Tc k1) 14 times....k12
43 S1pw T (cT) 3 times, k3....(k1 cTc 3T c) 14 times, k1....k11
44 S1pw T (cT) twice, k4....k1 (cT k1 Tc k1) 14 times....k11
45 S1pw T (cT) twice, k4....k2 c 3T (c k3 c 3T) 13 times, c k2....k10
46 S1pw TcT k5....k1 (Tc k1 cT k1) 14 times....k10
47 S1pw TcT k5....(c 3T c k1 cT) 14 times, cT....k8
48 S1pw k1 cTc k5....k1 (Tc k1 cT k1) 14 times....k9
49 S1pw k1 cTc k5....Tc k3 c (3T c k3 c) 13 times, T....k10
50 S1pw k1 (cT) twice, c k4....k1 (cT k1 Tc k1) 14 times....k10
51 S1pw k1 (cT) twice, c k4....(k1 cTc 3T c) 14 times, k1....k11
52 S1pw k1 (cT) 3 times, c k3....k1 (cT k1 Tc k1) 14 times....k11
53 S1pw k1 (cT) 3 times, c k3....k2 c 3T (c k3 c 3T) 13 times, c k2....k12
54 S1pw T (cT) 3 times, k3....k1 (Tc k1 cT k1) 14 times....k12
55 S1pw T (cT) 3 times, k3....(c 3T c k1 cT) 14 times, cT....k10
56 S1pw T (cT) twice, k4....k1 (Tc k1 cT k1) 14 times....k11
57 S1pw T (cT) twice, k4....Tc k3 c (3T c k3 c) 13 times, T....k10
58 S1pw TcT k5....k1 (cT k1 Tc k1) 14 times....k10

**Work as Rows 35 to 58 a further three times.**

This completes the RING STITCH & EDGING LACE SEQUENCE of 12 patterns and 8 scallops.

**BREAK ROWS & EDGING LACE SEQUENCE**

**ROW**

131 S1pw TcT k5....knit 85....k9

132 S1pw k1 cTc k5....purl 85....k9

133 S1pw k1 cTc k5....knit 85....k10

134 S1pw k1 (cT) twice, c k4....**KNIT 85**....k10

135 S1pw k1 (cT) twice, c k4....(cT) 43 times....k10

136 S1pw k1 (cT) 3 times, c k3....(cT) 43 times....k10

137 S1pw k1 (cT) 3 times, c k3....(cT) 43 times....k11

138 S1pw T (cT) 3 times, k3....**KNIT 85**....k12

139 S1pw T (cT) 3 times, k3....knit 85....k11

140 S1pw T (cT) twice, k4....purl 85....k11

141 S1pw T (cT) twice, k4....knit 85....k10

142 S1pw TcT k5....purl 85....k10

**PRINT of the WAVE & EDGING LACE SEQUENCE** (centre)

143 S1pw TcT k5....k1 cT k1, Tc Tc Tc (k1 T k3 T k1, c k1 c, Tc Tc) 5 times, k1, k2 cT....k9

144 S1pw k1 cTc k5....k1 cT k1, purl 77, k2 cT....k9

145 S1pw k1 cTc k5....k1 cT k1, Tc Tc Tc (k1 T k1 T k1, c k3 c, Tc Tc) 5 times, k1, k2 cT....k10

146 S1pw k1 (cT) twice, c k4....k1 cT k1, purl 77, k2 cT....k10

147 S1pw k1 (cT) twice, c k4....k1 cT k1, Tc Tc Tc (k1 s2kp k1, c k5 c, Tc Tc) 5 times, k1, k2 cT....K11

148 S1pw k1 (cT) 3 times, c k3....k1 cT k1, purl 77, k2 cT....k11

149 S1pw k1 (cT) 3 times, c k3....k1 cT k1, k1 cT cT (c k1 c, k1 T k3 T k1, cT cT) 5 times, cT k2 cT....k12

150 S1pw T (cT) 3 times, k3....k1 cT k1, purl 77, k2 cT....k12

151 S1pw T (cT) 3 times, k3....k1 cT k1, k1 cT cT (c k3 c, k1 T k1 T k1, cT cT) 5 times, cT k2 cT....k11

152 S1pw T (cT) twice, k4....k1 cT k1, purl 77, k2 cT....k11

153 S1pw T (cT) twice, k4....k1 cT k1, k1 cT cT (c k5 c, k1 s2kp k1, cT cT) 5 times, cT k2 cT....k10

154 S1pw TcT k5....k1 cT k1, purl 77, k2 cT....k10

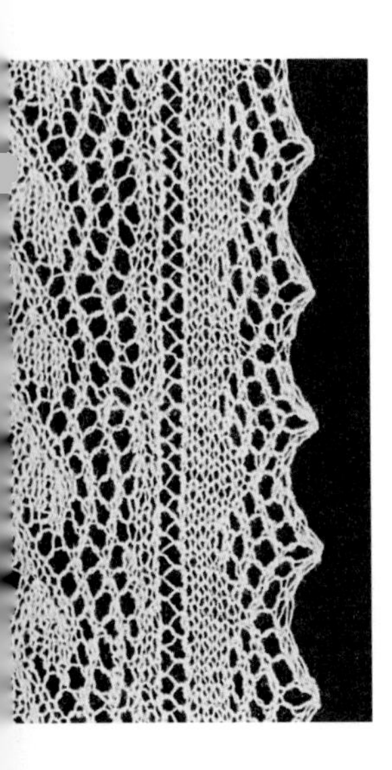

**Work as Rows 143 to 154 a further seventeen times,** giving 18 patterns.

**Row 359,** continue with the **BREAK ROWS & EDGING LACE, working as Rows 131 to 142 ONCE only.**

**Row 371,** continue with the **RING STITCH & EDGING LACE, working as Rows 35 to 58, THREE times,** giving 9 patterns of the RING STITCH and 6 scallops.

**ROW**

443 S1pw TcT k5....(k1 cTc 3T c) 14 times, k1....k9

444 S1pw k1 cTc k5....k1 (cT k1 Tc k1) 14 times....k9

445 S1pw k1 cTc k5....k2 c 3T (c k3 c 3T) 13 times, c k2....k10

446 S1pw k1 (cT) twice, c k4....k1 (Tc k1 cT k1) 14 times....k10

447 S1pw k1 (cT) twice, c k4....(c 3T c k1 cT) 14 times, cT....k10
**NOTE** : The last 'T' of rows 447, 455 and 464, takes up the first stitch of the edging lace.

448 S1pw k1 (cT) 3 times, c k3....k1 (Tc k1 cT k1) 14 times....k11

449 S1pw k1 (cT) 3 times, c k3....Tc k3 c (3T c k3 c) 13 times, T....k12

450 S1pw T (cT) 3 times, k3....k1 (cT k1 Tc k1) 14 times....k12

451 S1pw T (cT) 3 times, k3....(k1 cTc 3T c) 14 times, k1....k11

452 S1pw T (cT) twice, k4....k1 (cT k1 Tc k1) 14 times....k11

453 S1pw T (cT) twice, k4....k2 c 3T (c k3 c 3T) 13 times, c k2....k10

454 S1pw TcT k5....k1 (Tc k1 cT k1) 14 times....k10

455 S1pw TcT k5....(c 3T c k1 cT) 14 times, cT....k8

456 S1pw k1 cTc k5....k1 (Tc k1 cT k1) 14 times....k9

457 S1pw k1 cTc k5....Tc k3 c (3T c k3 c) 13 times, T....k10

458 S1pw k1 (cT) twice, c k4....k1 (cT k1 Tc k1) 14 times....k10

459 S1pw k1 (cT) twice, c k4....(k1 cTc 3T c) 14 times, k1....k11

460 S1pw k1 (cT) 3 times, c k3....k1 (cT k1 Tc k1) 14 times....k11

461 S1pw k1 (cT) 3 times, c k3....k2 c 3T (c k3 c 3T) 13 times, c k2....k12

462 S1pw T (cT) 3 times, k3....k1 (Tc k1 cT k1) 14 times....k12

Continue with corner turning as follows : —

463 + 464 S1pw T (cT) 3 times, k3, **TURN,** k11, and continue S1pw T (cT) twice, k4....(c 3T c k1 cT) 14 times, cT....k10

465 + 466 S1pw T (cT) twice, k4, **TURN,** k10, and continue S1pw TcT k5....k1 (Tc k1 cT k1) 14 times....k10

467 + 468 S1pw TcT k5, **TURN,** k9, and continue S1pw k1 cTc k5....Tc k3 c (3T c k3 c) 13 times, T....k9

469 + 470 S1pw k1 cTc k5, **TURN,** k10, and continue S1pw k1 (cT) twice, c k4....k1 (cT k1 Tc k1) 14 times....k10

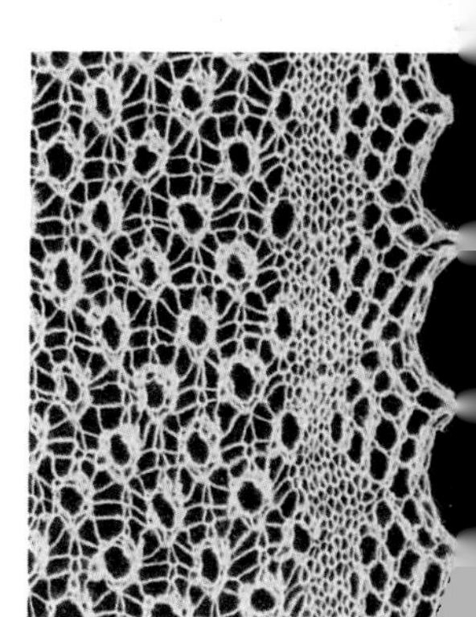

This completes the RING STITCH & EDGING LACE SEQUENCE.

Work the following six rows to complete the main body of the garment.

**ROW**

471 + 472 S1pw k1 (cT) twice, c k4, **TURN,** k11, and continue S1pw k1 (cT) 3 times, c k3....knit 85....k11

473 + 474 S1pw k1 (cT) 3 times, c k3, **TURN,** k12, and continue S1pw T (cT) 3 times, k3....purl 85....k12

475 + 476 S1pw T (cT) 3 times, k3, **TURN,** k11, and continue S1pw T (cT) twice, k4....knit 85....k11

With wrong side of work facing, continue working on Edging Lace ONLY from the 9th row (below).

Leave 85 stitches plus the 10 remaining edging stitches on a spare needle.

9th Row : S1pw T (cT) twice, k4 (10)

10th Row : S1pw knit to end.

11th Row : S1pw TcT, k5 (9)

12th Row : S1pw knit to end.

Continue with the edging lace sequence of 12 rows.

1st Row : S1pw k1 cTc, k5 (10)

**2nd and every alternate row : S1pw knit to end**

3rd Row : S1pw k1 (cT) twice, c k4 (11)

5th Row : S1pw k1 (cT) 3 times, c k3 (12)

7th Row : S1pw T (cT) 3 times, k3 (11)

9th Row : S1pw T (cT) twice, k4 (10)

11th Row : S1pw TcT, k5 (9)

12th Row : S1pw knit to end.

Work continuously until 14 scallops have been completed.

Pick up the 85 sts. from the straight edge and graft together with those on the spare needle and continue grafting edging stitches to complete

**TO DRESS THE GARMENT** : Wash **BY HAND ONLY** in lukewarm soapy water, squeezing gently. Rinse in lukewarm water. Roll up in a towel to absorb excess moisture. Stretch out to the approximate size 45″ x 15″ away from heat or sun, on a frame or pin out main garment and each scallop point on a white sheet and dry flat.

## ALTERNATIVE CENTRE PANEL

### CAT'S PAW & EDGING LACE SEQUENCE

**ROW**

143 S1pw TcT k5 .............................. k1 cT k1, k1 (k5 Tc k1 cT) 7 times, k6, k2 cT .... k9

144 S1pw k1 cTc k5 .......................... k1 cT k1, purl 77, k2 cT .... k9

145 S1pw k1 cTc k5 .......................... k1 cT k1, k2 (k3 Tc k3 cT) 7 times, k5, k2 cT .... k10

146 S1pw k1 (cT) twice, c k4 ......... k1 cT k1, purl 77, k2 cT .... k10

147 S1pw k1 (cT) twice, c k4 ......... k1 cT k1, k1 (k5 Tc k1 cT) 7 times, k6, k2 cT .... k11

148 S1pw k1 (cT) 3 times, c k3 ..... k1 cT k1, purl 77, k2 cT .... k11

149 S1pw k1 (cT) 3 times, c k3 ..... k1 cT k1, k1 (Tc k1 cT k5) 7 times, Tc k1 cT k1, k2 cT .... k12

150 S1pw T (cT) 3 times, k3 .......... k1 cT k1, purl 77, k2 cT .... k12

151 S1pw T (cT) 3 times, k3 .......... k1 cT k1, (Tc k3 cT k3) 7 times, Tc k3 cT, k2 cT .... k11

152 S1pw T (cT) twice, k4 ............. k1 cT k1, purl 77, k2 cT .... k11

153 S1pw T (cT) twice, k4 ............. k1 cT k1, k1 (Tc k1 cT k5) 7 times, Tc k1 cT k1, k2 cT .... k10

154 S1pw TcT k5 .............................. k1 cT k1, purl 77, k2 cT .... k10

Work as Rows 143 to 154 a further 17 times, giving 18 patterns.

**Continue with original pattern from row 359**

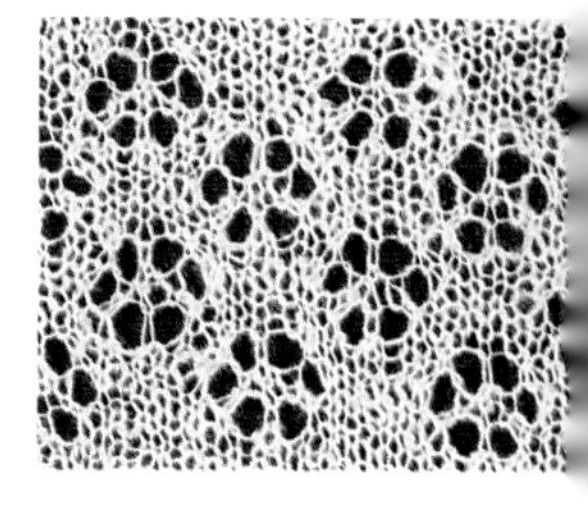

# *The Brora Black Shawl*

## A FINE LACE SHAWL KNITTED IN 1-PLY COBWEB WOOL

**Size — 52'' x 52'' (130cm x 130cm)**

**MATERIALS** : 8 hanks — 1-ply cobweb lace wool
1 circular needle — size 9 (3.75mm) — 30" (80cm) long
1 circular needle — size 9 (3.75mm) — 24" (60cm) long
5 double-ended needles — size 10 (3.25mm)

The main part of the shawl is knitted on the 30" No.9 circular needle. Towards the centre it will be necessary to change to the 24" needle in order not to stretch the work unduly. After row 147 the work is continued on the 5 double-ended, No.10 needles.

**BORDER LACE** : With No.9 needle cast on 10 stitches VERY loosely.

1st Row : Slip 1 purlwise, k1 cTc, k6 (11)

**2nd and every alternate row : Slip 1 purlwise, knit to end.**

3rd Row : Slip 1 purlwise, k1 (cT) twice, c k5 (12)

5th Row : Slip 1 purlwise, k1 (cT) 3 times, c k4 (13)

7th Row : Slip 1 purlwise, k1 (cT) 4 times, c k3 (14)

9th Row : Slip 1 purlwise, T (cT) 4 times, k3 (13)

11th Row : Slip 1 purlwise, T (cT) 3 times, k4 (12)

13th Row : Slip 1 purlwise, T (cT) twice, k5 (11)

15th Row : Slip 1 purlwise, TcT, k6 (10)

16th Row : Slip 1 purlwise, knit to end.

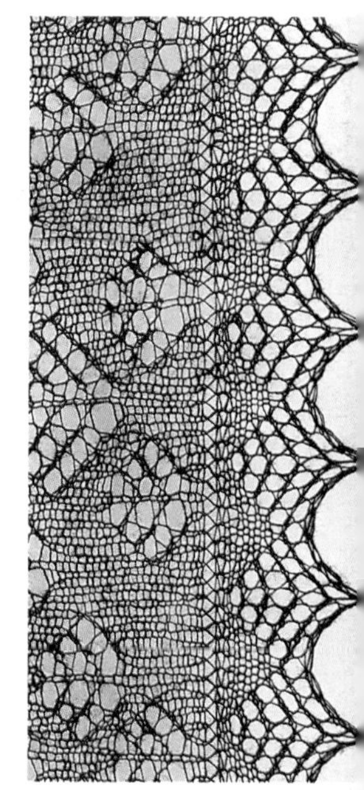

**These 16 rows form one scallop,** and are worked continuously until 104 scallops have been completed. Graft together the cast-on stitches and the stitches from the last row of the border lace.

**NOTE** : 104 scallops produce 832 stitches equalling 208 stitches per side.

*The Brora Black Shawl*

**From border lace — pick up 832 stitches, and (knit 208 sts. through back loops) 4 times, putting in marker threads at the end of each 208 sts. (i.e. at the four corners).** Additional marker threads in a different colour may be placed at the centre of each side to aid working if required.

**NOTE** : Instructions are given for **ONE SIDE ONLY** to be worked **FOUR TIMES CONTINUOUSLY,** up to and including Row 181.

Next row - T, knit 204, TB. (206)

Next row - T, knit 100, T, knit 100, TB. (203)

Knit one row. (203)

**NOTE** : Each pattern row consists of three parts; the beginning, the centre which is separated by dots and the end (which is the beginning knitted backwards.) From row 139 the centres are not shown separated.

**ROW**

1 T k7 (Tc k1 cT k5) 3 times, Tc k1 cT k9 (Tc k1 cT k7) twice,
Tc k1 cT k11....Tc k1 cT k7 Tc k1 cT....k11 Tc k1 cT,
(k7 Tc k1 cT) twice, k9 Tc k1 cT (k5 Tc k1 cT) 3 times, k7 TB (201)

**2 and every alternate row — knit**

3 T k5 (Tc k3 cT k3) 3 times, Tc k3 cT k7 (Tc k3 cT k5) twice,
Tc k3 cT k9....Tc k3 cT k5 Tc k3 cT....k9 Tc k3 cT,
(k5 Tc k3 cT) twice, k7 Tc k3 cT (k3 Tc k3 cT) 3 times, k5 TB (199)

5 T k3 (Tc Tc k1 cT cT k1) 3 times, Tc Tc k1 cT cT k5 (Tc Tc k1 cT cT k3) twice,
Tc Tc k1 cT cT k7....Tc Tc k1·cT cT k3 Tc Tc k1 cT cT....k7 Tc Tc k1 cT cT,
(k3 Tc Tc k1 cT cT) twice, k5 Tc Tc k1 cT cT (k1 Tc Tc k1 cT cT) 3 times, k3 TB (197)

7 T k3 (Tc k3 cT k3) 3 times, Tc k3 cT k7 (Tc k3 cT k5) twice,
Tc k3 cT k9....Tc k3 cT k5 Tc k3 cT....k9 Tc k3 cT,
(k5 Tc k3 cT) twice, k7 Tc k3 cT (k3 Tc k3 cT) 3 times, k3 TB (195)

9 T k3 (Tc k1 cT k5) 3 times, Tc k1 cT k9 (Tc k1 cT k7) twice,
Tc k1 cT k11....Tc k1 cT k7 Tc k1 cT....k11 Tc k1 cT,
(k7 Tc k1 cT) twice, k9 Tc k1 cT (k5 Tc k1 cT) 3 times, k3 TB (193)

11 T k7 (Tc k1 cT k5) twice (Tc k1 cT k9, Tc k1 cT k5) twice, Tc k1 cT k12....Tc k1 cT....
k12 Tc k1 cT (k5 Tc k1 cT, k9 Tc k1 cT) twice (k5 Tc k1 cT) twice, k7 TB (191)

13 T k5 (Tc k3 cT k3) twice (Tc k3 cT k7, Tc k3 cT k3) twice, Tc k3 cT k10....Tc k3 cT....
k10 Tc k3 cT (k3 Tc k3 cT, k7 Tc k3 cT) twice (k3 Tc k3 cT) twice, k5 TB (189)

*The Brora Black Shawl*

**ROW**

| ROW | | |
|---|---|---|
| 15 | T k3 (Tc Tc k1 cT cT k1) twice (Tc Tc k1 cT cT k5, Tc Tc k1 cT cT k1) twice, Tc Tc k1 cT cT k8....Tc Tc k1 cT cT....k8 Tc Tc k1 cT cT, (k1 Tc Tc k1 cT cT, k5 Tc Tc k1 cT cT) twice (k1 Tc Tc k1 cT cT) twice, k3 TB | (187) |
| 17 | T k3 (Tc k3 cT k3) twice (Tc k3 cT k7, Tc k3 cT k3) twice, Tc k3 cT k8....Tc Tc k3 cT cT.... k8 Tc k3 cT (k3 Tc k3 cT, k7 Tc k3 cT) twice (k3 Tc k3 cT) twice, k3 TB | (185) |
| 19 | T k3 (Tc k1 cT k5) twice (Tc k1 cT k9, Tc k1 cT k5) twice, Tc k1 cT k8....Tc Tc Tc k1 cT cT cT....k8 Tc k1 cT, (k5 Tc k1 cT, k9 Tc k1 cT) twice (k5 Tc k1 cT) twice, k3 TB | (183) |
| 21 | T k7, Tc k1 cT k5, Tc k1 cT k7 (Tc k1 cT k19) twice, Tc k1 cT k2....Tc Tc k3 cT cT.... k2 Tc k1 cT (k19 Tc k1 cT) twice, k7 Tc k1 cT, k5 Tc k1 cT, k7 TB | (181) |
| 23 | T k5, Tc k3 cT k3, Tc k3 cT k5 (Tc k3 cT k6, Tc k1 cT k6) twice, Tc k3 cT k2....Tc Tc k1 cT cT....k2 Tc k3 cT, (k6 Tc k1 cT, k6 Tc k3 cT) twice, k5 Tc k3 cT, k3 Tc k3 cT, k5 TB | (179) |
| 25 | T k3, Tc Tc k1 cT cT k1, Tc Tc k1 cT cT k3 (Tc Tc k1 cT cT k4, Tc k3 cT k4) twice, Tc Tc k1 cT cT k2....Tc k3 cT....k2 Tc Tc k1 cT cT, (k4 Tc k3 cT, k4 Tc Tc k1 cT cT) twice, k3 Tc Tc k1 cT cT, k1 Tc Tc k1 cT cT, k3 TB | (177) |
| 27 | T k3 (Tc k3 cT k3) twice (Tc Tc k3 cT cT k2, Tc Tc k1 cT cT k2) twice, Tc Tc k3 cT cT k2....Tc k1 cT....k2 Tc Tc k3 cT cT, (k2 Tc Tc k1 cT cT, k2 Tc Tc k3 cT cT) twice (k3 Tc k3 cT) twice, k3 TB | (175) |
| 29 | T k3, Tc k1 cT k5, Tc k1 cT k3 (Tc Tc Tc k1 cT cT cT k2, Tc k3 cT k2) twice, Tc Tc Tc k1 cT cT cT....k7....Tc Tc Tc k1 cT cT cT, (k2 Tc k3 cT, k2 Tc Tc Tc k1 cT cT cT) twice, k3 Tc k1 cT k5 Tc k1 cT, k3 TB | (173) |
| 31 | T k7, Tc k1 cT k7 (Tc Tc Tc k3 cT cT cT k2, Tc k1 cT k2) twice, Tc Tc Tc k3 cT cT cT....k5.... Tc Tc Tc k3 cT cT cT (k2 Tc k1 cT, k2 Tc Tc Tc k3 cT cT cT) twice, k7 Tc k1 cT, k7 TB | (171) |
| 33 | T k5, Tc k3 cT k5 (Tc Tc Tc Tc k1 cT cT cT cT k7) twice, Tc Tc Tc Tc k1 cT cT cT cT....k3.... Tc Tc Tc Tc k1 cT cT cT cT (k7 Tc Tc Tc Tc k1 cT cT cT cT) twice, k5 Tc k3 cT, k5 TB | (169) |
| 35 | T k3, Tc Tc k1 cT cT k5 (Tc Tc Tc k3 cT cT cT k9) twice, Tc Tc Tc k3 cT cT cT....k5.... Tc Tc Tc k3 cT cT cT (k9 Tc Tc Tc k3 cT cT cT) twice, k5 Tc Tc k1 cT cT, k3 TB | (167) |
| 37 | T k3, Tc k3 cT k7 (Tc Tc Tc k1 cT cT cT k3, Tc k1 cT k3) twice, Tc Tc Tc k1 cT cT cT....k7.... Tc Tc Tc k1 cT cT cT (k3 Tc k1 cT, k3 Tc Tc Tc k1 cT cT cT) twice, k7 Tc k3 cT, k3 TB | (165) |
| 39 | T k3, Tc k1 cT k9 (Tc Tc k3 cT cT k3, Tc k3 cT k3) twice, Tc Tc k3 cT cT k2....Tc k1 cT.... k2 Tc Tc k3 cT cT (k3 Tc k3 cT, k3 Tc Tc k3 cT cT) twice, k9 Tc k1 cT, k3 TB | (163) |

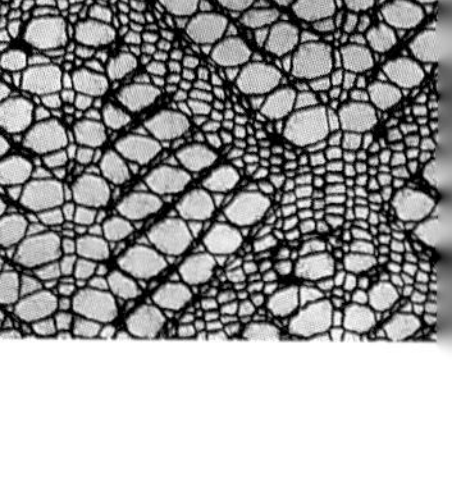

**ROW**

41 T k17 (Tc Tc k1 cT cT k3) 4 times, Tc Tc k1 cT cT k2....Tc k3 cT....
k2 Tc Tc k1 cT cT (k3 Tc Tc k1 cT cT) 4 times, k17 TB (161)

43 T k17 (Tc k3 cT k5) 4 times, Tc k3 cT k2....Tc Tc k1 cT cT....
k2 Tc k3 cT (k5 Tc k3 cT) 4 times, k17 TB. (159)

45 T k17 (Tc k1 cT k7) 4 times, Tc k1 cT k2....Tc Tc k3 cT cT....
k2 Tc k1 cT (k7 Tc k1 cT) 4 times, k17 TB (157)

47 T k70....Tc Tc Tc k1 cT cT cT....k70 TB (155)

49 T k68....Tc Tc Tc k3 cT cT cT....k68 TB (153)

51 T k6 (Tc k1 cT k3) twice, Tc k1 cT k5 (Tc k1 cT k7) twice,
Tc k1 cT k5....Tc Tc Tc Tc k1 cT cT cT cT....k5 Tc k1 cT,
(k7 Tc k1 cT) twice, k5 Tc k1 cT (k3 Tc k1 cT) twice, k6 TB (151)

53 T k4 (Tc k3 cT k1) twice, Tc k3 cT k3 (Tc k3 cT k5) twice,
Tc k3 cT k3....Tc Tc Tc Tc k3 cT cT cT cT....k3 Tc k3 cT,
(k5 Tc k3 cT) twice, k3 Tc k3 cT (k1 Tc k3 cT) twice, k4 TB (149)

55 T k2, Tc Tc k1 cTc s2kp cTc, k1, cTc s2kp cTc k1 cT cT, k1,
(Tc Tc k1 cT cT k3) 3 times....Tc Tc Tc Tc k1 cT cT cT cT....(k3 Tc Tc k1 cT cT) 3 times,
k1, Tc Tc k1 cTc s2kp cTc, k1 cTc s2kp cTc k1 cT cT, k2 TB (147)

57 T k2 (Tc k3 cT k1) twice, Tc k3 cT k3 (Tc k3 cT k5) 3 times....Tc Tc Tc k3 cT cT cT....
(k5 Tc k3 cT) 3 times, k3 Tc k3 cT (k1 Tc k3 cT) twice, k2 TB (145)

59 T k2 (Tc k1 cT k3) twice, Tc k1 cT k5 (Tc k1 cT k1) 4 times,
Tc k1 cT k7....Tc Tc Tc k1 cT cT cT....k7 Tc k1 cT,
(k1 Tc k1 cT) 4 times, k5 Tc k1 cT (k3 Tc k1 cT) twice, k2 TB (143)

61 T k5, Tc k1 cT k3, Tc k1 cT k14, Tc k3 cT k5, Tc k3 cT k6, Tc k1 cT k2....Tc Tc k3 cT cT....
k2 Tc k1 cT, k6 Tc k3 cT, k5 Tc k3 cT, k14 Tc k1 cT, k3 Tc k1 cT, k5 TB (141)

63 T k3, Tc k3 cT k1, Tc k3 cT k12, Tc Tc k1 cT cT k3, Tc Tc k1 cT cT k4,
Tc k3 cT k2....Tc Tc k1 cT cT....k2 Tc k3 cT,
k4 Tc Tc k1 cT cT, k3 Tc Tc k1 cT cT, k12 Tc k3 cT, k1 Tc k3 cT, k3 TB (139)

65 T k1, Tc Tc k1 cTc s2kp cTc k1 cT cT k12, Tc k3 cT k5, Tc k3 cT k4,
Tc Tc k1 cT cT k2....Tc k3 cT....k2 Tc Tc k1 cT cT,
k4 Tc k3 cT, k5 Tc k3 cT, k12 Tc Tc k1 cTc s2kp cTc k1 cT cT, k1 TB (137)

ROW

67 T k1, Tc k3 cT k1, Tc k3 cT k14 (Tc k1 cT k1) twice, Tc k1 cT k4,
Tc Tc k3 cT cT k2....Tc k1 cT....k2 Tc Tc k3 cT cT,
k4 Tc k1 cT (k1 Tc k1 cT) twice, k14 Tc k3 cT, k1 Tc k3 cT, k1 TB (135)

69 T k1, Tc k1 cT k3, Tc k1 cT k20, Tc k3 cT k8, Tc Tc Tc k1 cT cT cT....k7....
Tc Tc Tc k1 cT cT cT, k8 Tc k3 cT, k20 Tc k1 cT, k3 Tc k1 cT, k1 TB (133)

71 T k4, Tc k1 cT k23, Tc Tc k1 cT cT k6, Tc Tc Tc k3 cT cT cT....k5....
Tc Tc Tc k3 cT cT cT, k6 Tc Tc k1 cT cT, k23 Tc k1 cT, k4 TB (131)

73 T k2, Tc k3 cT k23, Tc k3 cT k8, Tc Tc Tc k1 cT cT cT....k7....
Tc Tc Tc k1 cT cT cT, k8 Tc k3 cT, k23 Tc k3 cT, k2 TB (129)

75 T, Tc Tc k1 cT cT k6, Tc k1 cT k5, Tc k1 cT k2, Tc k1 cT k10, Tc Tc k3 cT cT....k9....
Tc Tc k3 cT cT, k10 Tc k1 cT, k2 Tc k1 cT, k5 Tc k1 cT, k6 Tc Tc k1 cT cT, TB (127)

77 T, Tc k3 cT k6, Tc k3 cT k3, Tc k3 cT k17, Tc Tc k1 cT cT....k11....
Tc Tc k1 cT cT, k17 Tc k3 cT, k3 Tc k3 cT, k6 Tc k3 cT, TB (125)

79 T, Tc k1 cT k6, Tc Tc k1 cT cT k1, Tc Tc k1 cT cT k10, Tc k1 cT k2, Tc k3 cT k4....Tc k1 cT....
k4 Tc k3 cT, k2 Tc k1 cT, k10 Tc Tc k1 cT cT, k1 Tc Tc k1 cT cT, k6 Tc k1 cT, TB (123)

81 T k11, Tc k3 cT k3, Tc k3 cT k10, Tc k3 cT k2, Tc k1 cT k4....Tc k3 cT....
k4 Tc k1 cT, k2 Tc k3 cT, k10 Tc k3 cT, k3 Tc k3 cT, k11 TB (121)

83 T k11, Tc k1 cT k5, Tc k1 cT k10, Tc Tc k1 cT cT k9....Tc Tc k1 cT cT....
k9 Tc Tc k1 cT cT, k10 Tc k1 cT, k5 Tc k1 cT, k11 TB (119)

85 T k5 (Tc k1 cT k5) twice, Tc k1 cT k4, Tc Tc k3 cT cT k7....Tc Tc k3 cT cT....
k7 Tc Tc k3 cT cT, k4 Tc k1 cT (k5 Tc k1 cT) twice, k5 TB (117)

87 T k3 (Tc k3 cT k3) twice, Tc k3 cT k2, Tc Tc Tc k1 cT cT cT k5....Tc Tc Tc k1 cT cT cT....
k5 Tc Tc Tc k1 cT cT cT, k2 Tc k3 cT (k3 Tc k3 cT) twice, k3 TB (115)

89 T k1 (Tc Tc k1 cT cT k1) twice, Tc Tc k1 cT cT k2, Tc Tc k3 cT cT k7....Tc Tc k3 cT cT....
k7 Tc Tc k3 cT cT, k2 Tc Tc k1 cT cT (k1 Tc Tc k1 cT cT) twice, k1 TB (113)

91 T k1 (Tc k3 cT k3) twice, Tc k3 cT k4, Tc Tc k1 cT cT k9....Tc Tc k1 cT cT....
k9 Tc Tc k1 cT cT, k4 Tc k3 cT (k3 Tc k3 cT) twice, k1 TB (111)

93 T k1 (Tc k1 cT k5) twice, Tc k1 cT k6, Tc k3 cT k11....Tc k3 cT....
k11 Tc k3 cT, k6 Tc k1 cT (k5 Tc k1 cT) twice, k1 TB (109)

95 T k5, Tc k1 cT k5, Tc k1 cT k12, Tc k1 cT k3, Tc k1 cT k5....Tc k1 cT....
k5 Tc k1 cT, k3 Tc k1 cT, k12 Tc k1 cT, k5 Tc k1 cT, k5 TB (107)

# *The Brora Black Shawl*

| ROW | | |
|---|---|---|
| 97 | T k3, Tc k3 cT k3, Tc k3 cT k18, Tc k3 cT....k13....Tc k3 cT, k18 Tc k3 cT, k3 Tc k3 cT, k3 TB | (105) |
| 99 | T k1, Tc Tc k1 cT cT k1, Tc Tc k1 cT cT k16, Tc Tc k1 cT cT....k11.... Tc Tc k1 cT cT, k16 Tc Tc k1 cT cT, k1 Tc Tc k1 cT cT, k1 TB | (103) |
| 101 | T k1, Tc k3 cT k3, Tc k3 cT k16, Tc Tc k3 cT cT....k9.... Tc Tc k3 cT cT, k16 Tc k3 cT, k3 Tc k3 cT, k1 TB | (101) |
| 103 | T k1, Tc k1 cT k5, Tc k1 cT k16, Tc Tc Tc k1 cT cT cT....k7.... Tc Tc Tc k1 cT cT cT, k16 Tc k1 cT, k5 Tc k1 cT, k1 TB | (99) |
| 105 | T k32, Tc Tc k3 cT cT....k9....Tc Tc k3 cT cT. k32 TB | (97) |
| 107 | T k32, Tc Tc k1 cT cT....k11....Tc Tc k1 cT cT, k32 TB | (95) |
| 109 | T k5 (Tc k1 cT k5) twice, Tc k1 cT k2, Tc k3 cT k4....Tc k1 cT.... k4 Tc k3 cT, k2 Tc k1 cT (k5 Tc k1 cT) twice, k5 TB | (93) |
| 111 | T k3 (Tc k3 cT k3) twice, Tc k3 cT k2, Tc k1 cT k4....Tc k3 cT.... k4 Tc k1 cT, k2 Tc k3 cT (k3 Tc k3 cT) twice, k3 TB | (91) |
| 113 | T k1 (Tc Tc k1 cT cT k1) twice, Tc Tc k1 cT cT k9....Tc Tc k1 cT cT.... k9 Tc Tc k1 cT cT (k1 Tc Tc k1 cT cT) twice, k1 TB | (89) |
| 115 | T k1 (Tc k3 cT k3) twice, Tc k3 cT k9....Tc Tc k3 cT cT.... k9 Tc k3 cT (k3 Tc k3 cT) twice, k1 TB | (87) |
| 117 | T k1 (Tc k1 cT k5) twice, Tc k1 cT k4, Tc k1 cT k2....Tc Tc k1 cT cT.... k2 Tc k1 cT, k4 Tc k1 cT (k5 Tc k1 cT) twice, k1 TB | (85) |
| 119 | T k5, Tc k1 cT k5, Tc k1 cT k8, Tc k3 cT k2....Tc k3 cT.... k2 Tc k3 cT, k8 Tc k1 cT, k5 Tc k1 cT, k5 TB | (83) |
| 121 | T k3, Tc k3 cT k3, Tc k3 cT k6, Tc Tc k1 cT cT k2....Tc k1 cT.... k2 Tc Tc k1 cT cT, k6 Tc k3 cT, k3 Tc k3 cT, k3 TB | (81) |
| 123 | T k1, Tc Tc k1 cT cT k1, Tc Tc k1 cT cT k4, Tc Tc k3 cT cT....k7.... Tc Tc k3 cT cT, k4 Tc Tc k1 cT cT, k1 Tc Tc k1 cT cT, k1 TB | (79) |
| 125 | T k1, Tc k3 cT k3, Tc k3 cT k6, Tc Tc k1 cT cT k2....Tc k1 cT.... k2 Tc Tc k1 cT cT, k6 Tc k3 cT, k3 Tc k3 cT, k1 TB | (77) |
| 127 | T k1, Tc k1 cT k5, Tc k1 cT k8, Tc k3 cT k2....Tc k3 cT.... k2 Tc k3 cT, k8 Tc k1 cT, k5 Tc k1 cT, k1 TB | (75) |

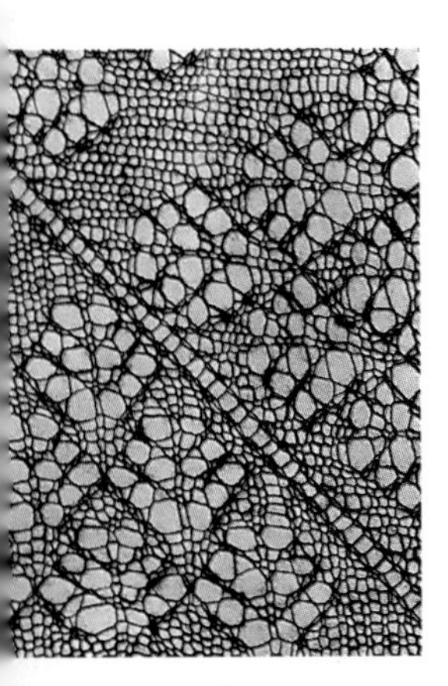

| ROW | | |
|---|---|---|
| 129 | T k5, Tc k1 cT k14, Tc k1 cT k2....Tc Tc k1 cT cT....k2 Tc k1 cT, k14 Tc k1 cT, k5 TB | (73) |
| 131 | T k3, Tc k3 cT k19....Tc Tc k3 cT cT....k19 Tc k3 cT, k3 TB | (71) |
| 133 | T k1, Tc Tc k1 cT cT k19....Tc Tc k1 cT cT....k19 Tc Tc k1 cT cT, k1 TB | (69) |
| 135 | T k1, Tc k3 cT k21....Tc k3 cT....k21 Tc k3 cT, k1 TB | (67) |
| 137 | T k1, Tc k1 cT k23....Tc k1 cT....k23 Tc k1 cT, k1 TB | (65) |
| 139 | T k5, Tc k1 cT k3 (Tc k1 cT k5) 3 times, Tc k1 cT, k3 Tc k1 cT, k5 TB | (63) |
| 141 | T k3, Tc k3 cT k1 (Tc k3 cT k3) 3 times, Tc k3 cT, k1 Tc k3 cT, k3 TB | (61) |
| 143 | T k1, Tc Tc k1 cTc s2kp cTc k1 cT cT k1 (Tc Tc k1 cT cT k1) twice, Tc Tc k1 cTc s2kp cTc k1 cT cT, k1 TB | (59) |
| 145 | T k1, Tc k3 cT k1 (Tc k3 cT k3) 3 times, Tc k3 cT, k1 Tc k3 cT, k1 TB | (57) |
| 147 | T k1, Tc k1 cT k3 (Tc k1 cT k5) 3 times, Tc k1 cT, k3 Tc k1 cT, k1 TB | (55) |

**CHANGE TO No.10 NEEDLES**

| | | |
|---|---|---|
| 149 | T k4, Tc k1 cT k14, Tc k1 cT, k14 Tc k1 cT, k4 TB | (53) |
| 151 | T k2, Tc k3 cT k12, Tc k3 cT, k12 Tc k3 cT, k2 TB | (51) |
| 153 | T, Tc Tc k1 cT cT k10, Tc Tc k1 cT cT, k10 Tc Tc k1 cT cT, TB | (49) |
| 155 | T, Tc k3 cT k12, Tc k3 cT, k12 Tc k3 cT, TB | (47) |
| 157 | T, Tc k1 cT k6, Tc k1 cT k3, Tc k1 cT, k3 Tc k1 cT, k6 Tc k1 cT, TB | (45) |
| 159 | T k9, Tc k3 cT k9 Tc k3 cT, k9 TB | (43) |
| 161 | T k7, Tc Tc k1 cT cT, k7, Tc Tc k1 cT cT, k7 TB | (41) |
| 163 | T k7, Tc k3 cT, k9, Tc k3 cT, k7 TB | (39) |
| 165 | T k7, Tc k1 cT k3, Tc k1 cT, k3 Tc k1 cT, k7 TB | (37) |
| 167 | T k13, Tc k3 cT, k13 TB | (35) |
| 169 | T k11, Tc Tc k1 cT cT, k11 TB | (33) |
| 171 | T k11, Tc k3 cT, k11 TB | (31) |

# *The Brora Black Shawl*

| ROW | | |
|---|---|---|
| 173 | T k11, Tc k1 cT, k11 TB | (29) |
| 175 | T k5, Tc k1 cT, k5, Tc k1 cT, k5 TB | (27) |
| 177 | T k3, Tc k3 cT, k3, Tc k3 cT, k3 TB | (25) |
| 179 | T k1, Tc Tc k1 cT cT, k1, Tc Tc k1 cT cT, k1 TB | (23) |
| 181 | T 3T c k3 c 3T, k1, 3T c k3 c 3T TB | (17) |

**NOTE** : Work round continuously from row 182. The total count for the round will be shown ( ). The last **'T'** of row 182 takes up the first stitch of row 183.

| | | |
|---|---|---|
| 182 | k16 T, k15 T, k15 T, k15 T | (64) |
| 183 | (3T c k1 c 3T k1, 3T c k1 c 3T k1) four times | (48) |
| 184 | Knit 48 | |
| 185 | Knit 48 | |
| 186 | Knit 48 | |
| 187 | (k3 Tc k1 cT k4) four times (48 sts.) | |
| 188 | Knit 48 | |
| 189 | (k2 Tc k3 cT k3) four times (48 sts.) | |
| 190 | Knit 49 **(over-running into row 191)** | |
| 191 | (k2 Tc k1 cT k2 s2kp) four times (40 sts.) | |
| 192 | Knit 40 | |
| 193 | T all round (20 sts.) | |
| 194 | T all round (10 sts.) | |

**DRAW UP LOOSELY AND FASTEN OFF SECURELY**

**TO DRESS SHAWL** : Wash **BY HAND ONLY** in lukewarm soapy water, squeezing gently. Rinse in lukewarm water. Roll up in a towel to absorb excess moisture. Stretch out to dry to a perfect square 52" x 52" approx., away from heat or sun, on a shawl frame or pin out scallops at points on to a white sheet, and dry flat.

# *The Gibbie Shawl*

## A FINE LACE SHAWL KNITTED IN 1-PLY COBWEB WOOL

### Size — 50'' x 50'' (125cm x 125cm)

**MATERIALS** : 7 hanks — 1-ply cobweb lace Shetland wool
1 circular needle — size 9 (3.75mm) — 30″ (80cm) long
1 circular needle — size 9 (3.75mm) — 24″ (60cm) long
5 double-ended needles — size 10 (3.25mm)

The main part of the shawl is knitted on the 30″ No.9 circular needle. Towards the centre it will be necessary to change to the 24″ needle in order not to stretch the work unduly. After row 155 the work is continued on the 5 double-ended, No.10 needles.

## *The Gibbie Shawl*

**BORDER LACE** : With No.9 needle cast on 10 stitches VERY loosely.

1st Row : Slip 1 purlwise, k1 cTc, k6 (11)

**2nd and every alternate row : Slip 1 purlwise, knit to end.**

3rd Row : Slip 1 purlwise, k1 (cT) twice, c k5 (12)

5th Row : Slip 1 purlwise, k1 (cT) 3 times, c k4 (13)

7th Row : Slip 1 purlwise, k1 (cT) 4 times, c k3 (14)

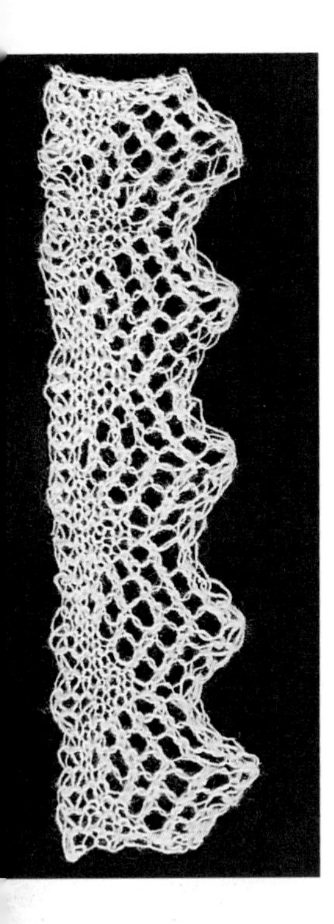

9th Row : Slip 1 purlwise, T (cT) 4 times, k3 (13)

11th Row : Slip 1 purlwise, T (cT) 3 times, k4 (12)

13th Row : Slip 1 purlwise, T (cT) twice, k5 (11)

15th Row : Slip 1 purlwise, TcT, k6 (10)

16th Row : Slip 1 purlwise, knit to end.

**These 16 rows form one scallop,** and are worked continuously until 96 scallops have been completed. Graft together the cast-on stitches and the stitches from the last row of the border lace.

**NOTE** : 96 scallops produce 768 stitches equalling 192 stitches per side.

**From border lace — pick up 768 stitches, and (knit 192 sts. through back loops) 4 times, putting in marker threads at the end of each 192 sts. (i.e. at the four corners).**

**Purl one row. (768 sts.)**

**NOTE** : The **'K1'** at the beginning of each pattern row is the corner stitch and is constant throughout. From now on instructions are given for **ONE SIDE ONLY** to be worked **FOUR TIMES CONTINUOUSLY**, up to and including Row 181.

| ROW | | |
|---|---|---|
| 1 | K1 TB, k11 (Tc k1 cT k11) 11 times, T | (190) |
| **2** | **and every alternate row — purl** | |
| 3 | K1 TB, k9 (Tc k3 cT k9) 11 times, T | (188) |
| 5 | K1 TB, k9 (Tc k1 cT k11) 10 times, Tc k1 cT, k9 T | (186) |
| 7 | K1 TB, k181, T | (184) |
| 9 | K1 TB, k179, T | (182) |
| 11 | K1 TB, k14 (Tc k1 cT k11) 9 times, Tc k1 cT, k14 T | (180) |
| 13 | K1 TB, k5 (Tc k1 cT k2 Tc k3 cT k2) 10 times, Tc k1 cT, k5 T | (178) |
| 15 | K1 TB, k3 (Tc k3 cT k2 Tc k1 cT k2) 10 times, Tc k3 cT, k3 T | (176) |
| 17 | K1 TB, k1 (Tc Tc k1 cT cT k7) 10 times, Tc Tc k1 cT cT, k1 T | (174) |
| 19 | K1 3TB, cTc k3 cT cT k5 (Tc Tc k3 cT cT k5) 9 times, Tc Tc k3 cTc 3T | (172) |
| 21 | K1 3TB, cTc k1 cT cT cT, k3 (Tc Tc Tc, k1, cT cT cT, k3) 9 times, Tc Tc Tc, k1, cTc 3T | (170) |
| 23 | K1 3TB, c k3 cT cT cT, k1 (Tc Tc Tc, k3, cT cT cT, k1) 9 times, Tc Tc Tc, k3, c 3T | (168) |
| 25 | K1 TB, k4 (cT cT, c s2kp c, Tc Tc k5) 9 times, cT cT, c s2kp c, Tc Tc, k4 T | (166) |
| 27 | K1 TB, k4 (cT cT k1 Tc Tc k7) 9 times, cT cT k1 Tc Tc, k4 T | (164) |
| 29 | K1 TB, k4 (cT, c s2kp c, Tc k9) 9 times, cT, c s2kp c, Tc, k4 T | (162) |
| 31 | K1 TB, k4 (cT k1 Tc, k3, Tc k1 cT, k3) 9 times, cT k1 Tc, k4 T | (160) |
| 33 | K1 TB, k4 (c s2kp c, k3, Tc k3 cT, k3) 9 times, c s2kp c, k4 T | (158) |
| 35 | K1 TB, k8 (Tc Tc k1 cT cT k7) 8 times, Tc Tc k1 cT cT, k8 T | (156) |
| 37 | K1 TB, k8 (Tc k3 cT k9) 8 times, Tc k3 cT, k8 T | (154) |
| 39 | K1 TB, k8 (Tc k1 cT k11) 8 times, Tc k1 cT, k8 T | (152) |
| 41 | K1 TB, k15 (Tc k1 cT k11) 7 times, Tc k1 cT, k15 T | (150) |

| ROW | | |
|---|---|---|
| 43 | K1 TB, k13 (Tc k3 cT k9) 7 times, Tc k3 cT, k13 T | (148) |
| 45 | K1 TB, k13 (Tc k1 cT k11) 7 times, Tc k1 cT, k13 T | (146) |
| 47 | K1 TB, k20 (Tc k1 cT k11) 6 times, Tc k1 cT, k20 T | (144) |
| 49 | K1 TB, k18 (Tc k3 cT k9) 6 times, Tc k3 cT, k18 T | (142) |
| 51 | K1 TB, k16 (Tc Tc k1 cT cT k7) 6 times, Tc Tc k1 cT cT, k16 T | (140) |
| 53 | K1 TB, k9 (Tc k1 cT k2 Tc k3 cT k2) 7 times, Tc k1 cT, k9 T | (138) |
| 55 | K1 TB, k7 (Tc k3 cT k2 Tc k1 cT k2) 7 times, Tc k3 cT, k7 T | (136) |
| 57 | K1 TB, k5 (Tc Tc k1 cT cT k7) 7 times, Tc Tc k1 cT cT, k5 T | (134) |
| 59 | K1 TB, k3 (Tc Tc k3 cT cT k5) 7 times, Tc Tc k3 cT cT, k3 T | (132) |
| 61 | K1 TB, k1 (Tc Tc Tc, k1, cT cT cT, k3) 7 times, Tc Tc Tc, k1, cT cT cT, k1 T | (130) |
| 63 | K1 3TB, cT cT c k3 (cT cT cT, k1, Tc Tc Tc, k3) 7 times, cT cT c 3T | (128) |
| 65 | K1 3TB, cTc k5 (cT cT, c s2kp c, Tc Tc k5) 7 times, cTc 3T | (126) |
| 67 | K1 3TB, c k7 (cT cT k1 Tc Tc k7) 7 times, c 3T | (124) |
| 69 | K1 TB, k8 (cT, c s2kp c, Tc k9) 6 times, cT, c s2kp c, Tc, k8 T | (122) |
| 71 | K1 TB, k8 (cT k1 Tc k3 Tc k1 cT k3) 6 times, cT k1 Tc, k8 T | (120) |
| 73 | K1 TB, k8 (c s2kp c k3 Tc k3 cT k3) 6 times, c s2kp c, k8 T | (118) |
| 75 | K1 TB, k14 (Tc k1 cT k11) 5 times, Tc k1 cT, k14 T | (116) |
| 77 | K1 TB, k53, Tc k1 cT, k53 T | (114) |
| 79 | K1 TB, k51, Tc k3 cT, k51 T | (112) |
| 81 | K1 TB, k3 (Tc k1 cT k11) 6 times, Tc k1 cT, k3 T | (110) |
| 83 | K1 TB, k1 (Tc k3 cT k9) twice, Tc k3 cT k25 (Tc k3 cT k9) twice, Tc k3 cT, k1 T | (108) |
| 85 | K1 TB, k1 (Tc k1 cT k11) 6 times, Tc k1 cT, k1 T | (106) |

ROW

| | | |
|---|---|---|
| 87 | K1 TB, k47, Tc k3 cT, k47 T | (104) |
| 89 | K1 TB, k47, Tc k1 cT, k47 T | (102) |
| 91 | K1 TB, k10 (Tc k1 cT k3 Tc k1 cT k19) twice, Tc k1 cT k3 Tc k1 cT, k10 T | (100) |
| 93 | K1 TB, k8 (Tc k3 cT k1 Tc k3 cT k17) twice, Tc k3 cT k1 Tc k3 cT, k8 T | (98) |
| 95 | K1 TB, k8 (Tc k1 cT k3 Tc k1 cT k19) twice, Tc k1 cT k3 Tc k1 cT, k8 T | (96) |
| 97 | K1 TB, k3 (Tc k1 cT k3 Tc k1 cT k3 Tc k1 cT k11) twice, Tc k1 cT k3 Tc k1 cT k3 Tc k1 cT, k3 T | (94) |
| 99 | K1 TB, k1 (Tc k3 cT k1 Tc k3 cT k1 Tc k3 cT k9) twice, Tc k3 cT k1 Tc k3 cT k1 Tc k3 cT, k1 T | (92) |
| 101 | K1 TB, k1 (Tc k1 cT k3 Tc k1 cT k3 Tc k1 cT k11) twice, Tc k1 cT k3 Tc k1 cT k3 Tc k1 cT, k1 T | (90) |
| 103 | K1 TB, k4 (Tc k1 cT k3 Tc k1 cT k19) twice, Tc k1 cT k3 Tc k1 cT, k4 T | (88) |
| 105 | K1 TB, k2 (Tc k3 cT k1 Tc k3 cT k17) twice, Tc k3 cT k1 Tc k3 cT, k2 T | (86) |
| 107 | K1 TB, k2 (Tc k1 cT k3 Tc k1 cT k19) twice, Tc k1 cT k3 Tc k1 cT, k2 T | (84) |
| 109 | K1 TB, k5 Tc k1 cT k27, Tc k1 cT k27, Tc k1 cT, k5 T | (82) |
| 111 | K1 TB, k3 Tc k3 cT k25, Tc k3 cT k25, Tc k3 cT, k3 T | (80) |
| 113 | K1 TB, k3 Tc k1 cT k27, Tc k1 cT k27, Tc k1 cT, k3 T | (78) |
| 115 | K1 TB, k73 T | (76) |
| 117 | K1 TB, k11 Tc k1 cT k3 Tc k1 cT, k9 Tc k1 cT k9, Tc k1 cT k3 Tc k1 cT, k11 T | (74) |
| 119 | K1 TB, k9 Tc k3 cT k1 Tc k3 cT, k7 Tc k3 cT k7, Tc k3 cT k1 Tc k3 cT, k9 T | (72) |
| 121 | K1 TB, k9 Tc k1 cT k3 Tc k1 cT, k9 Tc k1 cT k9, Tc k1 cT k3 Tc k1 cT, k9 T | (70) |
| 123 | K1 TB, k4 Tc k1 cT k3 Tc k1 cT k3 Tc k1 cT k15, Tc k1 cT k3 Tc k1 cT k3 Tc k1 cT, k4 T | (68) |
| 125 | K1 TB, k2 Tc k3 cT k1 Tc k3 cT k1 Tc k3 cT k13, Tc k3 cT k1 Tc k3 cT k1 Tc k3 cT, k2 T | (66) |
| 127 | K1 TB, k2 (Tc k1 cT k3) twice (Tc k1 cT k5) twice (Tc k1 cT k3) twice, Tc k1 cT, k2 T | (64) |
| 129 | K1 TB, k5 Tc k1 cT k3 Tc k1 cT, k8 Tc k3 cT k8, Tc k1 cT k3 Tc k1 cT, k5 T | (62) |



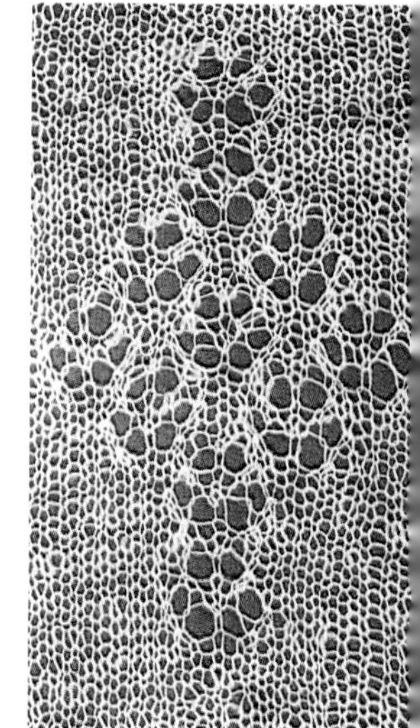

| ROW | | |
|---|---|---|
| 131 | K1 TB, k3 Tc k3 cT k1 Tc k3 cT, k8 Tc k1 cT k8, Tc k3 cT k1 Tc k3 cT, k3 T | (60) |
| 133 | K1 TB, k3 (Tc k1 cT k3 Tc k1 cT k5) twice, Tc k1 cT k3 Tc k1 cT, k3 T | (58) |
| 135 | K1 TB, k6 Tc k1 cT, k8 Tc k3 cT k1 Tc k3 cT k8, Tc k1 cT, k6 T | (56) |
| 137 | K1 TB, k4 Tc k3 cT, k8 Tc k1 cT k3 Tc k1 cT k8, Tc k3 cT, k4 T | (54) |
| 139 | K1 TB, k4 Tc k1 cT, k5 Tc k1 cT, k3 Tc k1 cT, k3 Tc k1 cT, k5 Tc k1 cT, k4 T | (52) |
| 141 | K1 TB, k12 Tc k3 cT k1, Tc k3 cT k1, Tc k3 cT, k12 T | (50) |
| 143 | K1 TB, k12 Tc k1 cT k3, Tc k1 cT k3, Tc k1 cT, k12 T | (48) |
| 145 | K1 TB, k7 Tc k1 cT k3, Tc k1 cT k3, Tc k1 cT k3, Tc k1 cT, k7 T | (46) |
| 147 | K1 TB, k5 Tc k3 cT k1, Tc k3 cT k1, Tc k3 cT k1, Tc k3 cT, k5 T | (44) |
| 149 | K1 TB, k5 Tc k1 cT k3, Tc k1 cT k3, Tc k1 cT k3, Tc k1 cT, k5 T | (42) |
| 151 | K1 TB, k8 Tc k1 cT k3, Tc k1 cT k3, Tc k1 cT, k8 T | (40) |
| 153 | K1 TB, k6 Tc k3 cT k1, Tc k3 cT k1, Tc k3 cT, k6 T | (38) |
| 155 | K1 TB, k6 Tc k1 cT k3, Tc k1 cT k3, Tc k1 cT, k6 T | (36) |

**CHANGE TO No. 10 NEEDLES**

| | | |
|---|---|---|
| 157 | K1 TB, k9 Tc k1 cT, k3 Tc k1 cT, k9 T | (34) |
| 159 | K1 TB, k7 Tc k3 cT, k1 Tc k3 cT, k7 T | (32) |
| 161 | K1 TB, k7 Tc k1 cT, k3 Tc k1 cT, k7 T | (30) |
| 163 | K1 TB, k10 Tc k1 cT, k10 T | (28) |
| 165 | K1 TB, k8 Tc k3 cT, k8 T | (26) |
| 167 | K1 TB, k8 Tc k1 cT, k8 T | (24) |
| 169 | K1 TB, k19 T | (22) |

| ROW | | |
|---|---|---|
| 171 | K1 TB, k2 Tc k1 cT, k3 Tc k1 cT, k2 T | (20) |
| 173 | K1 TB, Tc k3 cT, k1, Tc k3 cT, T | (18) |
| 175 | K1 TB, Tc k1 cT, k3, Tc k1 cT, T | (16) |
| 177 | K1 TB, k3 Tc k1 cT, k3 T | (14) |
| 179 | K1 TB, k1 Tc k3 cT, k1 T | (12) |
| 181 | K1 TB, k1 Tc k1 cT, k1 T | (10) |
| 182 | Purl all round. (40 sts.) | |
| 183 | (K1 TB, k5 T) 4 times. (32 sts.) | |
| 184 | Purl all round. | |
| 185 | T all round. (16 sts.) | |
| 186 | Purl all round. | |
| 187 | T all round. (8 sts.) | |

**DRAW UP LOOSELY AND FASTEN OFF SECURELY**

**TO DRESS SHAWL :** Wash **BY HAND ONLY** in lukewarm soapy water, squeezing gently. Rinse in lukewarm water. Roll up in a towel to absorb excess moisture. Stretch out to dry to a perfect square 50" x 50" approx., away from heat or sun, on a shawl frame or pin out scallops at points on to a white sheet, and dry flat.

# *Baby's Lace Jacket & Bonnet*

**A FINE LACE JACKET & BONNET KNITTED IN 1-PLY COBWEB WOOL**

**Size — TO FIT BABY UP TO 6 MONTHS**

**MATERIALS** : 3 hanks — 1-ply cobweb lace Shetland wool
1 circular needle — size 10 (3.25mm) — 24" (60cm) long
1 circular needle — size 11 (3.00mm) — 24" (60cm) long
or 1 pair of needles — size 10 (3.25mm)
1 pair of needles — size 11 (3.00mm)
Nylon press fasteners for neck & waist fastening.
Ribbon — 2.5 metres x 9mm for bonnet,
jacket waist & neck
1.0 metre x 3mm for jacket cuffs

## JACKET INSTRUCTIONS

With No.10 needle cast on 169 stitches **VERY** loosely (two-needle method).

Knit three rows.

Next row — Knit 4, purl 161, knit 4

Continue, working the 8 rows of the Horseshoe stitch sequence 8 times (64 rows), **keeping the 4 sts. at each end in garter stitch for the front borders.** (The garter stitch borders are maintained throughout and are included in the row detail, separated from the main body by a row of dots).

**HORSESHOE STITCH SEQUENCE**

**ROW**

5 K4....k1 (c k3 s2kp k3 c k1) 16 times....k4

**6 and every alternate row — K4....purl to last 4 sts....k4**

7 K4....k2 (c k2 s2kp k2 c k3) 15 times, c k2 s2kp k2 c k2....k4

9 K4....k3 (c k1 s2kp k1 c k5) 15 times, c k1 s2kp k1 c k3....k4

11 K4....k4 (c s2kp c k7) 15 times, c s2kp c k4....k4

12 K4....purl to last 4 sts....k4

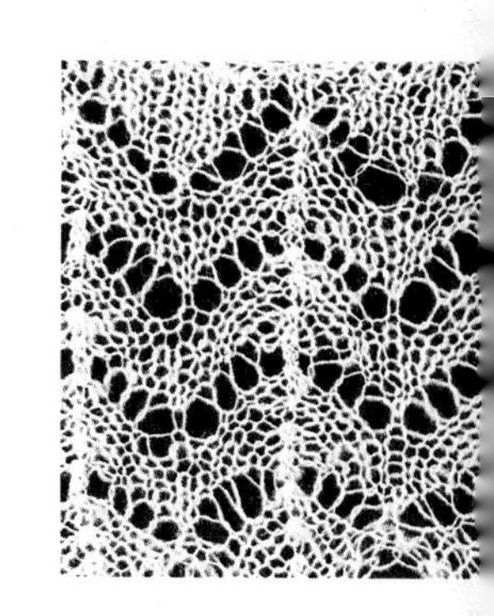

*Baby's Lace Jacket & Bonnet*

**WAIST INSTRUCTIONS**

**ROW**

69 Knit 4....knit 161....knit 4

70 Knit 4....purl 161....knit 4

71 Knit 4....knit 161....knit 4

72 Knit 4....knit 161....knit 4

73 Make holes for ribbon — K4....k2 (cT k2) to last 7 sts., cT k1....k4

74 Knit 4....knit 161....knit 4

**CHANGE TO No.11 NEEDLE**

75 Knit 4....knit 161....knit 4

76 Knit 4....purl 161....knit 4

77 Knit 4....knit 161....knit 4

78 Knit 4....purl 161....knit 4

**DIAMOND BEAD STITCH SEQUENCE**

79 K4....k8 (Tc k1 cT k15) 7 times, Tc k1 cT k8....k4 (169)

80 K4....p7 (Tc k3 cT p13) 7 times, Tc k3 cT p7....k4

81 K4....k5 (Tc k1 cT k1, Tc k1 cT k9) 7 times, Tc k1 cT k1, Tc k1 cT k5....k4

82 K4....p4 (Tc k3 c s2kp c k3 cT p7) 7 times, Tc k3 c s2kp c k3 cT p4....k4

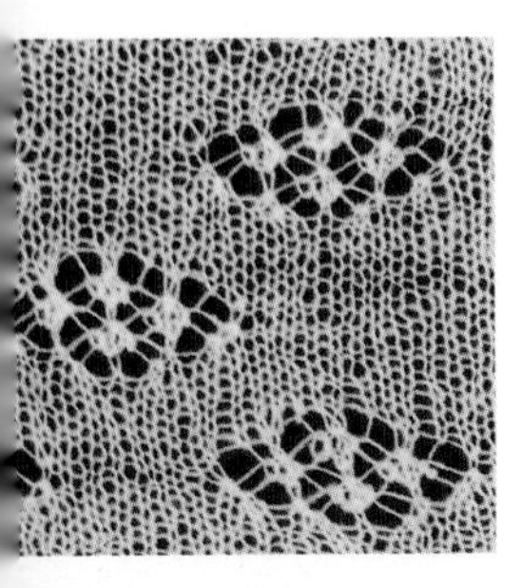

83 K4....k5 (cT k1 Tc k1, cT k1 Tc k9) 7 times, cT k1 Tc k1, cT k1 Tc k5....k4

84 K4....p6 (c s2kp c k3, c s2kp c p11) 7 times, c s2kp c k3, c s2kp c p6....k4

85 K4....k8 (cT k1 Tc k15) 7 times, cT k1 Tc k8....k4

86 K4....p9 (c s2kp c p17) 7 times, c s2kp c p9....k4

87 K4....k39, T k79 T, k39....k4 (167)

88 Knit 4....purl 159....knit 4

**DIVIDE FOR FRONTS & BACK**

**ROW**

89 K4....k18 Tc k1 cT k14, cast off 4 sts., k16 (incl. st. from cast off), (Tc k1 cT k15) twice, Tc k1 cT k16, cast off 4 sts., k14 (incl. st. from cast off), Tc k1 cT k18....k4 i.e. border 4, right front 37, back 77, left front 37, border 4. (159)

**LEFT FRONT**

With wrong side of work facing, continue working on LEFT-HAND FRONT ONLY, leaving remaining stitches on spare needle or thread. (Fronts and back details will commence from row 90 in each case).

| | | |
|---|---|---|
| 90 | K4....p17, Tc k3 cT p13 | (4 + 37) |
| 91 | Cast off 2 sts., k9, Tc k1 cT k1, Tc k1 cT k15....k4 | (35 + 4) |
| 92 | K4....p14, Tc k3 c s2kp c k3 cT, p8 | (4 + 35) |
| 93 | T k7, cT k1 Tc k1, cT k1 Tc k15....k4 | (34 + 4) |
| 94 | K4....p16, c s2kp c k3, c s2kp c p7 PT | (4 + 33) |
| 95 | T k8, cT k1 Tc k18....k4 | (32 + 4) |
| 96 | K4....p19, c s2kp c p8 PT | (4 + 31) |
| 97 | K31....k4 | |
| 98 | K4....p31 | |
| 99 | K18, Tc k1 cT k8....k4 | |
| 100 | K4....p7, Tc k3 cT p17 | |
| 101 | K5, Tc k1 cT k5, Tc k1 cT k1, Tc k1 cT k5....k4 | |
| 102 | K4....p4, Tc k3 c s2kp c k3 cT p3, Tc k3 cT p4 | |
| 103 | K5, cT k1 Tc k5, cT k1 Tc k1, cT k1 Tc k5....k4 | |
| 104 | K4....p6, c s2kp c k3, c s2kp c p7, c s2kp c p6 | |
| 105 | K18, cT k1 Tc k8....k4 | |
| 106 | K4....p9, c s2kp c p19 | |
| 107 | K31....k4 | |

| ROW | | |
|---|---|---|
| 108 | K4....p31 | |
| 109 | K10, Tc k1 cT k16....k4 | |
| 110 | K4....p15, Tc k3 cT p9 | |
| 111 | K10, cT k1 Tc k16....k4 | |
| 112 | K4....p17, c s2kp c p11 | |
| 113 | Knit 28, leaving remaining 7 sts. on a pin. | (28) |
| 114 | Cast off 3 sts. purlwise, purl to end. | (25) |
| 115 | Knit 25 | (25) |
| 116 | Cast off 2 sts. purlwise, purl to end. | (23) |
| 117 | K21, T | (22) |
| 118 | PT, purl 20 | (21) |
| 119 | K19, T | (20) |
| 120 | PT, purl 18 | (19) |
| 121 | K17, T | (18) |

Break off wool, leaving sufficient for grafting at the shoulder. Leave stitches on a thread ready for dressing garment flat.

**BACK**

With wrong side of work facing, rejoin wool at LEFT-HAND armhole, and commence working on BACK.

| | | |
|---|---|---|
| 90 | P15 (Tc k3 cT p13) twice, Tc k3 cT p15 | (77) |
| 91 | Cast off 2 sts., k11 (Tc k1 cT k1, Tc k1 cT, k9) twice, Tc k1 cT k1, Tc k1 cT k13 | (75) |
| 92 | Cast off 2 sts. purlwise, p10 (Tc k3 c s2kp c k3 cT p7) twice, Tc k3 c s2kp c k3 cT p10 | (73) |
| 93 | T k9 (cT k1 Tc k1, cT k1 Tc k9) twice, cT k1 Tc k1, cT k1 Tc k9 TB | (71) |
| 94 | PT p9 (c s2kp c k3, c s2kp c p11) twice, c s2kp c k3, c s2kp c p9 T | (69) |
| 95 | T k10 (cT k1 Tc k15) twice, cT k1 Tc k10 TB | (67) |
| 96 | PT p10 (c s2kp c p17) twice, c s2kp c p10 T | (65) |

| ROW | | |
|---|---|---|
| 97 | Knit | (65) |
| 98 | Purl | |
| 99 | K20 Tc k1 cT k15 Tc k1 cT k20 | |
| 100 | P19 Tc k3 cT k13 Tc k3 cT p19 | |
| 101 | K17 Tc k1 cT k1 Tc k1 cT k9, Tc k1 cT k1 Tc k1 cT k17 | |
| 102 | P16 Tc k3 c s2kp c k3 cT p7, Tc k3 c s2kp c k3 cT p16 | |
| 103 | K17 cT k1 Tc k1 cT k1 Tc k9, cT k1 Tc k1 cT k1 Tc k17 | |
| 104 | P18 c s2kp c k3, c s2kp c p11, c s2kp c k3, c s2kp c p18 | |
| 105 | K20 cT k1 Tc k15 cT k1 Tc k20 | |
| 106 | P21 c s2kp c p17 c s2kp c p21 | |
| 107 | Knit | |
| 108 | Purl | |
| 109 | K10 (Tc k1 cT k15) twice, Tc k1 cT k10 | |
| 110 | P9 (Tc k3 cT p13) twice, Tc k3 cT p9 | |
| 111 | K7 (Tc k1 cT k1, Tc k1 cT k9) twice, Tc k1 cT k1, Tc k1 cT k7 | |
| 112 | P6 (Tc k3 c s2kp c k3 cT p7) twice, Tc k3 c s2kp c k3 cT p6 | |
| 113 | K7 (cT k1 Tc k1, cT k1 Tc k9) twice, cT k1 Tc k1, cT k1 Tc k7 | |
| 114 | P8 (c s2kp c k3 c s2kp c p11) twice, c s2kp c k3 c s2kp c p8 | |
| 115 | K10 (cT k1 Tc k15) twice, cT k1 Tc k10 | |
| 116 | P11 (c s2kp c p17) twice, c s2kp c p11 | |
| 117 | Knit | |
| 118 | Purl | |
| 119 | Knit | (65) |

Break off wool and leave stitches on a thread ready for dressing garment flat.

**RIGHT FRONT**

With wrong side of work facing, rejoin wool at RIGHT-HAND armhole, and commence working on RIGHT FRONT.

**ROW**

| | | |
|---|---|---|
| 90 | Cast off 2 sts. purlwise, p11 Tc k3 cT p17....k4 | (35 + 4) |
| 91 | K4....k15 Tc k1 cT k1, Tc k1 cT, k9 | (4 + 35) |
| 92 | PT, p6 Tc k3 c s2kp c k3 cT p14....k4 | (34 + 4) |
| 93 | K4....k15 cT k1 Tc k1, cT k1 Tc k6 T | (4 + 33) |
| 94 | PT, p6 c s2kp c k3, c s2kp c p16....k4 | (32 + 4) |
| 95 | K4....k18 cT k1 Tc k7 T | (4 + 31) |
| 96 | P9, c s2kp c p19....k4 | (31 + 4) |
| 97 | K4....k31 | |
| 98 | P31....k4 | |
| 99 | K4....k8 Tc k1 cT k18 | |
| 100 | P17, Tc k3 cT p7....k4 | |
| 101 | K4....k5 Tc k1 cT k1, Tc k1 cT k5, Tc k1 cT k5 | |
| 102 | P4, Tc k3 cT p3, Tc k3 c s2kp c k3 cT p4....k4 | |
| 103 | K4....k5 cT k1 Tc k1, cT k1 Tc k5, cT k1 Tc k5 | |
| 104 | P6, c s2kp c p7, c s2kp c k3, c s2kp c p6....k4 | |
| 105 | K4....k8 cT k1 Tc k18 | |
| 106 | P19, c s2kp c p9....k4 | |
| 107 | K4....k31 | |
| 108 | P31....k4 | |
| 109 | K4....k16 Tc k1 cT k10 | |
| 110 | P9 Tc k3 cT p15....k4 | |
| 111 | K4....k16 cT k1 Tc k10 | |
| 112 | P11, c s2kp c p17....k4 | |

**ROW**

| | | |
|---|---|---|
| 113 | K4....k31 | (35) |
| 114 | Purl 28, leaving remaining 7 sts. on a pin. | (28) |
| 115 | Cast off 3 sts., knit to end. | (25) |
| 116 | Purl 25 | (25) |
| 117 | Cast off 2 sts., knit to end. | (23) |
| 118 | P21, PT | (22) |
| 119 | T, k20 | (21) |
| 120 | P19, PT | (20) |
| 121 | T, k18 | (19) |
| 122 | P17, PT | (18) |

Break off wool and leave stitches on a thread ready for dressing garment flat.

**SLEEVES** (both alike) :

With No.10 needle cast on 51 stitches **VERY** loosely (two-needle method).

Knit three rows.

Work the 8 rows of the Horseshoe stitch sequence.

**HORSESHOE STITCH SEQUENCE**

**ROW**

1 K1 (c k3 s2kp k3 c k1) 5 times.

**2 and every alternate row — purl**

3 K2 (c k2 s2kp k2 c k3) 4 times, c k2 s2kp k2 c k2

5 K3 (c k1 s2kp k1 c k5) 4 times, c k1 s2kp k1 c k3

7 K4 (c s2kp c k7) 4 times, c s2kp c k4

8 Purl

*Baby's Lace Jacket & Bonnet*

**SLEEVES** (continued)

Knit one row. Purl one row. Knit two rows. Purl one row. Knit two rows.

Next row — make holes for ribbon — K3 (cT k2) to end.

Knit two rows. Purl one row. Increase row — K3 (make one, k5) 9 times, make one, k3 (61)

Purl one row.

Continue, working the 4 rows of the Bead stitch sequence 11 times (44 rows).

**BEAD STITCH SEQUENCE**

1 K2 (c s2kp c k3) 9 times, c s2kp c k2

2 K1 T (c k1 cT k1 T) 9 times, c k1 cT k1

3 Tc (k3 c s2kp c) 9 times, k3 cT

4 K1 c (T k1 Tc k1 c) 9 times, T k1 Tc k1

**ARMHOLE DECREASE,** (keeping pattern in sequence) :

Cast off 2 sts., at the beginning of the next 4 rows, then, (53)

Next two rows — 'T' at the beginning and end of each. (49)

Next row — Tc (k3 c s2kp c) 7 times, k3 cT

Next row — K1 c (T k1 Tc k1 c) 7 times, T k1 Tc k1

Continue, working the 4 rows of the Bead stitch sequence **(AS BELOW)** 7 times (28 rows).

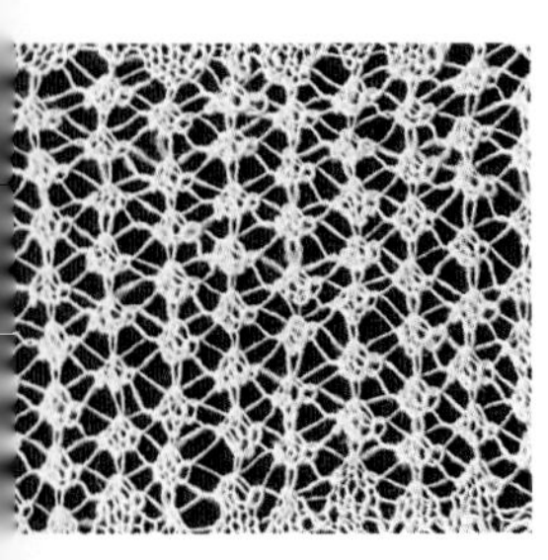

**BEAD STITCH SEQUENCE**

1 K2 (c s2kp c k3) 7 times, c s2kp c k2

2 K1 T (c k1 cT k1 T) 7 times, c k1 cT k1

3 Tc (k3 c s2kp c) 7 times, k3 cT

4 K1 c (T k1 Tc k1 c) 7 times, T k1 Tc k1

**SHAPE TOP OF SLEEVE** :

Cast off 8 sts. at the beginning of the next 3 rows, then, (25)

Cast off 7 sts. purl to end. (18)

Next row — (T) whole row. (9)

Cast off remaining stitches.

**NOTE** : It is recommended that all pieces of the garment be dressed at this stage, before sewing up.

**TO DRESS GARMENT** : Wash main part of garment and sleeves separately **BY HAND ONLY** in lukewarm soapy water, squeezing gently. Rinse in lukewarm water. Roll up in a towel to absorb excess moisture. Stretch and pin out to shape, away from heat or sun and dry flat.
Dress sleeves and lay flat, pinned out to shape.

After dressing, graft together the shoulder seams. Sew up sleeve seams and fit into armholes, gathering the top as necessary.

**NECKBAND** :

With right side of work facing, transfer 7 'pin' stitches to needle, then rejoin wool at RIGHT-HAND FRONT neck and pick up and knit 16 sts. from RIGHT-HAND SIDE neck, 29 sts. from BACK, and 16 sts. from LEFT-HAND SIDE neck and 7 'pin' stitches from LEFT-HAND front. **(Total 75 sts.)**

Work 9 rows in stocking stitch.

**CAST OFF LOOSELY**

Fold neckband in half and lightly stitch in position on wrong side.
Attach 9mm ribbon for neckband ties, but **DO NOT THREAD THROUGH NECK.**
Thread ribbon through waist (9mm), and cuffs (3mm).
Sew on nylon press fasteners at neck and waist, if required.

## BONNET INSTRUCTIONS

With No.10 needle cast on 121 stitches **VERY** loosely (two-needle method).

Knit three rows.

Continue, working the 8 rows of the Horseshoe stitch sequence.

**HORSESHOE STITCH SEQUENCE**

**ROW**

4 K1 (c k3 s2kp k3 c k1) 12 times.

**5 and every alternate row — purl to end.**

6 K2 (c k2 s2kp k2 c k3) 11 times, c k2 s2kp k2 c k2.

8 K3 (c k1 s2kp k1 c k5) 11 times, c k1 s2kp k1 c k3.

10 K4 (c s2kp c k7) 11 times, c s2kp c k4.

11 Purl to end.

Knit one row. Purl one row. Knit two rows. Purl one row.

Next row — decrease row — k7 (T k1) to last 9 sts., T k7 (85)

Purl one row. Knit one row. Purl one row.

Continue, working the 4 rows of the Bead stitch sequence 16 times (64 rows) to row 84.

**BEAD STITCH SEQUENCE**

21 K2 (c s2kp c k3) 13 times, c s2kp c k2

22 K1 T (c k1 cT k1 T) 13 times, c k1 cT k1

23 Tc (k3 c s2kp c) 13 times, k3 cT

24 K1 c (T k1 Tc k1 c) 13 times, T k1 Tc k1

85 Decrease row — T k7 T (k4 T) 11 times, k8 (72)

Purl one row. Knit one row. Purl one row.

**ROW**

| | | |
|---|---|---|
| 89 | (K7 T) to end. | (64) |
| **90 and every alternate row — purl to end.** | | |
| 91 | (K6 T) to end. | (56) |
| 93 | (K5 T) to end. | (48) |
| 95 | (K4 T) to end. | (40) |
| 97 | (K3 T) to end. | (32) |
| 99 | (K2 T) to end. | (24) |
| 101 | (K1 T) to end. | (16) |
| 103 | (T) to end. | (8) |
| 104 | Purl to end. | (8) |

**DRAW UP AND SECURE STITCHES**

Join back seams for 6cms.

Dress garment, using a bowl or balloon to shape to a suitable size.

To form upstand, stitch together the 8th and 12th pattern rows. Turn up scallop edge to form a brim and stitch lightly into place at the front edge. The upstand and brim may be pressed lightly with a WARM iron over a protective cloth.

# *Cobweb Lace Wrap*

**KNITTED IN 1-PLY COBWEB WOOL**

**Size — 46'' x 46'' x 66'' (115cm x 115cm x 165cm)**

**MATERIALS** : 7 hanks — 1-ply cobweb lace wool
1 circular needle — size 10 (3.25mm) — 30" (80cm) long
1 circular needle — size 11 (3.00mm) — 30" (80cm) long

This triangular wrap is a useful and attractive accessory for evening wear or for chilly days — enough to offer warmth to one's shoulders without excess weight. When knitted in either black or white, it is ideal for formal occasions, such as weddings, garden parties, theatre visits, as it enhances a garment of any colour.

The wrap is knitted in two main stitch patterns — Roundels and Diamond Chain, and features a scallop edge worked in a variety of sizes.

The garment is worked in one piece, which avoids the sewing up of seams.

*Cobweb Lace Wrap*

## BORDER LACE

With No.10 needle :

Cast on 19 sts. **VERY** loosely.

Knit one row.

Starter row — S1pw TcT, knit to end (18)

Next row — S1pw, knit to end

The border lace for this wrap is worked from the 48 row sequence knitting the rows as detailed below to create 29 scallops of varying size. The 15th (centre) scallop is a double scallop with two points.

After completing the 29th scallop, cast off **VERY LOOSELY**.

| **TO KNIT SCALLOP** | **: ROWS WORKED (incl.)** |
|---|---|
| 1 | 1 — 18 then 31 — 48 |
| 2 and 16 | 1 — 48 |
| 3, 9, 17, 23 | 1 — 18 then 31 — 48 |
| 4, 10, 18, 24 | 1 — 14 then 35 — 48 |
| 5, 11, 19, 25 | 1 — 10 then 39 — 48 |
| 6, 12, 20, 26 | 1 — 14 then 35 — 48 |
| 7, 13, 21, 27 | 1 — 18 then 31 — 48 |
| 8, 14, 22, 28 | 1 — 48 |
| 29 | 1 — 18 then 31 — 48 |
| 15 (centre scallop has 2 points). | 1 — 20, 29 — 40, then 9 — 20, 29 — 48 |

**SCALLOP ROWS**

| | |
|---|---|
| 1st Row : S1pw k1 cTc, k14 | (19) |
| **2nd and every alternate row : S1pw, knit to end.** | |
| 3rd Row : S1pw k1 (cT) twice, c k13 | (20) |
| 5th Row : S1pw k1 (cT) 3 times, c k12 | (21) |
| 7th Row : S1pw k1 (cT) 4 times, c k11 | (22) |
| 9th Row : S1pw k1 (cT) 5 times, c k10 | (23) |
| 11th Row : S1pw k1 (cT) 6 times, c k9 | (24) |
| 13th Row : S1pw k1 (cT) 7 times, c k8 | (25) |
| 15th Row : S1pw k1 (cT) 8 times, c k7 | (26) |
| 17th Row : S1pw k1 (cT) 9 times, c k6 | (27) |
| 19th Row : S1pw k1 (cT) 10 times, c k5 | (28) |
| 21st Row : S1pw k1 (cT) 11 times, c k4 | (29) |
| 23rd Row : S1pw k1 (cT) 12 times, c k3 | (30) |
| 25th Row : S1pw (Tc) 12 times, T k3 | (29) |
| 27th Row : S1pw (Tc) 11 times, T k4 | (28) |
| 29th Row : S1pw (Tc) 10 times, T k5 | (27) |
| 31st Row : S1pw (Tc) 9 times, T k6 | (26) |
| 33rd Row : S1pw (Tc) 8 times, T k7 | (25) |
| 35th Row : S1pw (Tc) 7 times, T k8 | (24) |
| 37th Row : S1pw (Tc) 6 times, T k9 | (23) |
| 39th Row : S1pw (Tc) 5 times, T k10 | (22) |
| 41st Row : S1pw (Tc) 4 times, T k11 | (21) |
| 43rd Row : S1pw (Tc) 3 times, T k12 | (20) |
| 45th Row : S1pw (Tc) twice, T k13 | (19) |
| 47th Row : S1pw TcT, k14 | (18) |
| 48th Row : S1pw, knit to end. | |

**NOTE** : The 29 scallops produce 509 stitches.

**From border lace — pick up 509 stitches along the straight edge, and starting at the RIGHT-HAND side,**

**Knit one row through back loops.**

Next row — S1pw, knit to end.
Next row — S1pw, knit to end.
Next row — S1pw, purl to last 14 sts., and leave these on a safety pin, and continue.

**ROW**

1 S1pw k2 (Tc k1 cTB k5) 47 times, Tc k1 cTB k3, and leave remaining 14 sts. on a safety pin. (481)

**2nd, 4th, 6th and 8th rows : Slip 1 knitwise, purl to end.**

3 S1pw k1 (Tc k3 cTB k3) 47 times, Tc k3 cTB k2

5 S1pw k2 (cTB k1 Tc k5) 47 times, cTB k1 Tc k3

7 S1pw k3 (c s2kp c k7) 47 times, c s2kp c k4 (481)

9 S1pw, knit to end.

10 S1pw, knit to end.

11 S1pw T, knit 475, TB k1 (479)

12 Slip 1 knitwise, purl to end.

**PLEASE READ THE FOLLOWING NOTES CAREFULLY BEFORE PROCEEDING FURTHER**

Complete pattern rows are worked from RIGHT-HAND side panel, through CENTRE panel and LEFT-HAND panel. A decrease, of one stitch, is worked at the beginning and end of each side panel on the pattern rows only and every alternate row is worked in purl.

The pattern is fully detailed for each complete row, with the centre panel separated at each end by dots in the pattern to aid the knitter. The stitch counts are given for the three constituent panels.

During the next row, coloured marker threads should be placed at the beginning and end of the centre panel.

# *Cobweb Lace Wrap*

**ROW**

1 S1pw T k4 Tc k1 cTB k7,
*** (k6 cTB k2 cTB k6, k3, Tc k1 cTB k3 Tc k1 cTB, k3) 4 times, k6 cTB k2 cTB k6 *** (202)
k2 Tc k1 cTB k9, TB k1....k3 (Tc k1 cTB k5) 6 times, Tc k1 cTB k3....k1 T k9 Tc k1 cTB k2, + (71)
repeat *** — *** , k7 Tc k1 cTB k4, TB k1 + (202)

**2 and every alternate row — Slip 1 knitwise, purl to end.**

3 S1pw T k2 Tc k3 cTB k6,
*** (k4 Tc k1 cTB k2 cTB k5, k2, Tc k3 cTB k1 Tc k3 cTB, k2) 4 times, k4 Tc k1, cTB k2 cTB k5 *** (200)
k1 Tc k3 cTB k7, TB k1....k2 (Tc k3 cTB k3) 6 times, Tc k3 cTB k2....k1 T k7 Tc k3 cTB k1, + (71)
repeat *** — *** , k6 Tc k3 cTB k2, TB k1 + (200)

5 S1pw T k2 cTB k1 Tc k7,
*** (k3 Tc k3 cTB k2 cTB k4, k3, cTB k1 Tc k3 cTB k1 Tc, k3) 4 times, k3 Tc k3, cTB k2 cTB k4 *** (198)
k2 cTB k1 Tc k7, TB k1....k3 (cTB k1 Tc k5) 6 times, cTB k1 Tc k3....k1 T k7 cTB k1 Tc k2, + (71)
repeat *** — *** , k7 cTB k1 Tc k2, TB k1 + (198)

7 S1pw T k2, c s2kp c k8,
*** (k2 Tc k2 Tc k1, cTB k2 cTB k3, k4, c s2kp c k5, c s2kp c, k4) 4 times,
k2 Tc k2 Tc k1, cTB k2 cTB k3 *** (196)
k3 c s2kp c k7, TB k1....k4 (c s2kp c k7) 6 times, c s2kp c k4....k1 T k7 c s2kp c k3, + (71)
repeat *** — *** , k8 c s2kp c k2, TB k1 (196)

9 S1pw *** T k12 (k1 Tc k2 Tc k3, cTB k2 cTB k2, k7, Tc k1 cTB k7) 4 times,
k1 Tc k2 Tc k3, cTB k2 cTB k2, k12 TB k1 *** (194)
....k8 (Tc k1 cTB k5) 6 times, k3....k1, repeat *** — *** +(71) +(194)

11 S1pw *** T k11 (k3 cTB k2 cTB, cTc k2 TcT k1, k6 Tc k3 cTB k6) 4 times,
k3 cTB k2 cTB, cTc k2 TcT k1, k11 TB k1 *** (192)
....k7 (Tc k3 cTB k3) 6 times, k4....k1, repeat *** — *** +(71) +(192)

13 S1pw *** T k10 (k4 cTB k2 c s2kp c k2 Tc k3, k7, cTB k1 Tc k7) 4 times,
k4 cTB k2 c s2kp c k2, Tc k3, k10 TB k1 *** (190)
....k8 (cTB k1 Tc k5) 6 times, k3....k1, repeat *** — *** +(71) +(190)

15 S1pw *** T k9 (k5 cTB k2 cTB k1, Tc k4, k8, c s2kp c k8) 4 times,
k5 cTB k2 cTB k1, Tc k4, k9 TB k1 *** (188)
....k9 (c s2kp c k7) 6 times, k2....k1, repeat *** — *** +(71) +(188)

16 Slip 1 knitwise, purl to end.

**PATTERN 'D' : DIAMOND CHAIN STITCH**

1st Row K6, cTB k2 cTB, k6

**2nd and every alternate row — purl.**

3rd Row K4, Tc k1, cTB k2 cTB, k5

5th Row K3, Tc k3, cTB k2 cTB, k4

7th Row K2, Tc k2 Tc k1, cTB k2 cTB, k3

9th Row K1, Tc k2 Tc k3, cTB k2 cTB, k2

11th Row K3, cTB k2 cTB, cTc k2 TcT, k1

13th Row K4, cTB k2 c s2kp c k2, Tc, k3

15th Row K5, cTB k2 cTB k1, Tc, k4

16th Row Purl

**PATTERN 'R' : ROUNDEL STITCH**

1st Row K3, Tc k1 cTB, k3, Tc k1 cTB, k3

**2nd and every alternate row — purl.**

3rd Row K2, Tc k3 cTB, k1, Tc k3 cTB, k2

5th Row K3, cTB k1 Tc, k3, cTB k1 Tc, k3

7th Row K4, c s2kp c, k5, c s2kp c, k4

9th Row K7, Tc k1 cTB, k7

11th Row K6, Tc k3 cTB, k6

13th Row K7, cTB k1 Tc, k7

15th Row K8, c s2kp c, k8

16th Row Purl



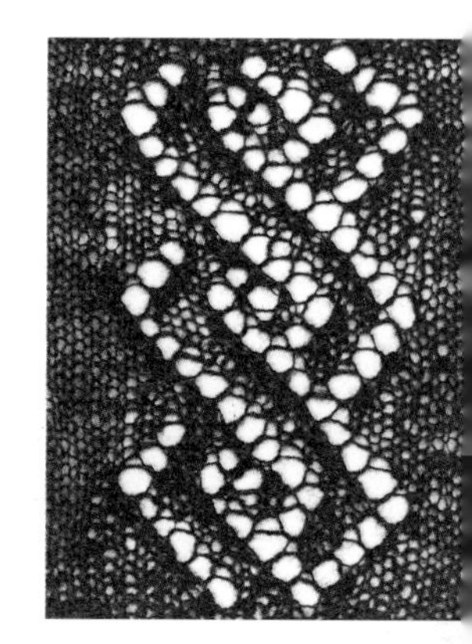

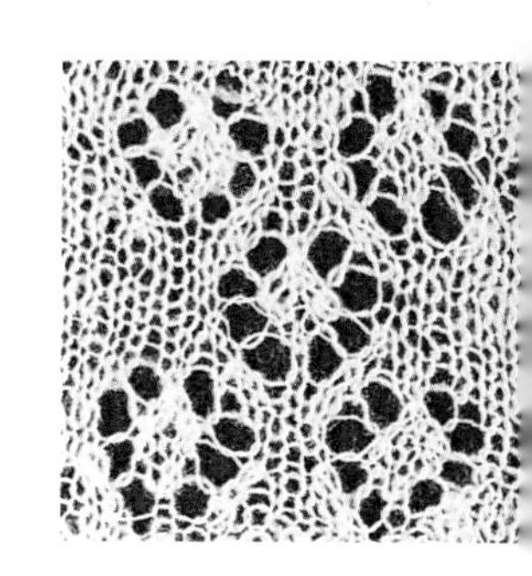

**WORKING INSTRUCTIONS** (continued).

**NOTE** : From Row 17, the stitch sequences 'D' & 'R' in the side panels refer to the detailed rows given in the Diamond Chain and Roundel sequences shown above.

| ROW | | | |
|---|---|---|---|
| 17 | S1pw *** T k8, Row 1 of D, R, D, R, D, R, D, R, D, k8 TB k1 *** | | (186) |
| | ....k3 (Tc k1 cTB k5) 6 times, Tc k1 cTB k3....k1, repeat *** — *** | +(71) | +(186) |
| 19 | S1pw *** T k7, Row 3 of D, R, D, R, D, R, D, R, D, k7 TB k1 *** | | (184) |
| | ....k2 (Tc k3 cTB k3) 6 times, Tc k3 cTB k2....k1, repeat *** — *** | +(71) | +(184) |
| 21 | S1pw *** T k6, Row 5 of D, R, D, R, D, R, D, R, D, k6 TB k1 *** | | (182) |
| | ....k3 (cTB k1 Tc k5) 6 times, cTB k1 Tc k3....k1, repeat *** — *** | +(71) | +(182) |
| 23 | S1pw *** T k5, Row 7 of D, R, D, R, D, R, D, R, D, k5 TB k1 *** | | (180) |
| | ....k4 (c s2kp c k7) 6 times, c s2kp c k4....k1, repeat *** — *** | +(71) | +(180) |
| 25 | S1pw *** T k4, Row 9 of D, R, D, R, D, R, D, R, D, k4 TB k1 *** | | (178) |
| | ....k8 (Tc k1 cTB k5) 6 times, k3....k1, repeat *** — *** | +(71) | +(178) |
| 27 | S1pw *** T k3, Row 11 of D, R, D, R, D, R, D, R, D, k3 TB k1 *** | | (176) |
| | ....k7 (Tc k3 cTB k3) 6 times, k4....k1, repeat *** — *** | +(71) | +(176) |
| 29 | S1pw *** T k2, Row 13 of D, R, D, R, D, R, D, R, D, k2 TB k1 *** | | (174) |
| | ....k8 (cTB k1 Tc k5) 6 times, k3....k1, repeat *** — *** | +(71) | +(174) |
| 31 | S1pw *** T k1, Row 15 of D, R, D, R, D, R, D, R, D, k1 TB k1 *** | | (172) |
| | ....k9 (c s2kp c k7) 6 times, k2....k1, repeat *** — *** | +(71) | +(172) |
| 33 | S1pw *** T k6, cTB k2 cTB k6, Row 1 of R, D, R, D, R, D, R, k6 cTB k2 cTB, k6 TB k1 *** | | (170) |
| | ....k3 (Tc k1 cTB k5) 6 times, Tc k1 cTB k3....k1, repeat *** — *** | +(71) | +(170) |
| 35 | S1pw *** T k6, cTB k2 cTB k5, Row 3 of R, D, R, D, R, D, R, k7 cTB k2 cTB, k4 TB k1 *** | | (168) |
| | ....k2 (Tc k3 cTB k3) 6 times, Tc k3 cTB k2....k1, repeat *** — *** | +(71) | +(168) |
| 37 | S1pw *** T k6, cTB k8, Row 5 of R, D, R, D, R, D, R, k8 cTB, k6 TB k1 *** | | (166) |
| | ....k3 (cTB k1 Tc k5) 6 times, cTB k1 Tc k3....k1, repeat *** — *** | +(71) | +(166) |
| 39 | S1pw *** T k6, cTB k7, Row 7 of R, D, R, D, R, D, R, k9 cTB, k4 TB k1 *** | | (164) |
| | ....k4 (c s2kp c k7) 6 times, c s2kp c k4....k1, repeat *** — *** | +(71) | +(164) |
| 41 | S1pw *** T k6, cTB k6, Row 9 of R, D, R, D, R, D, R, k10 cTB, k2 TB k1 *** | | (162) |
| | ....k8 (Tc k1 cTB k5) 6 times, k3....k1, repeat *** — *** | +(71) | +(162) |
| 43 | S1pw *** T k13, Row 11 of R, D, R, D, R, D, R, k13 TB k1 *** | | (160) |
| | ....k7 (Tc k3 cTB k3) 6 times, k4....k1, repeat *** — *** | +(71) | +(160) |
| 45 | S1pw *** T k12, Row 13 of R, D, R, D, R, D, R, k12 TB k1 *** | | (158) |
| | ....k8 (cTB k1 Tc k5) 6 times, k3....k1, repeat *** — *** | +(71) | +(158) |
| 47 | S1pw *** T k11, Row 15 of R, D, R, D, R, D, R, k11 TB k1 *** | | (156) |
| | ....k9 (c s2kp c k7) 6 times, k2....k1, repeat *** — *** | +(71) | +(156) |

| ROW | | |
|---|---|---|
| 49 | S1pw *** T k10, Row 1 of R, D, R, D, R, D, R, k10 TB k1 ***<br>....k3 (Tc k1 cTB k5) 6 times, Tc k1 cTB k3....k1, repeat *** — *** | (154)<br>+(71) +(154) |
| 51 | S1pw *** T k9, Row 3 of R, D, R, D, R, D, R, k9 TB k1 ***<br>....k2 (Tc k3 cTB k3) 6 times, Tc k3 cTB k2....k1, repeat *** — *** | (152)<br>+(71) +(152) |
| 53 | S1pw *** T k8, Row 5 of R, D, R, D, R, D, R, k8 TB k1 ***<br>....k3 (cTB k1 Tc k5) 6 times, cTB k1 Tc k3....k1, repeat *** — *** | (150)<br>+(71) +(150) |
| 55 | S1pw *** T k7, Row 7 of R, D, R, D, R, D, R, k7 TB k1 ***<br>....k4 (c s2kp c k7) 6 times, c s2kp c k4....k1, repeat *** — *** | (148)<br>+(71) +(148) |
| 57 | S1pw *** T k6, Row 9 of R, D, R, D, R, D, R, k6 TB k1 ***<br>....k8 (Tc k1 cTB k5) 6 times, k3....k1, repeat *** — *** | (146)<br>+(71) +(146) |
| 59 | S1pw *** T k5, Row 11 of R, D, R, D, R, D, R, k5 TB k1 ***<br>....k7 (Tc k3 cTB k3) 6 times, k4....k1, repeat *** — *** | (144)<br>+(71) +(144) |
| 61 | S1pw *** T k4, Row 13 of R, D, R, D, R, D, R, k4 TB k1 ***<br>....k8 (cTB k1 Tc k5) 6 times, k3....k1, repeat *** — *** | (142)<br>+(71) +(142) |
| 63 | S1pw *** T k3, Row 15 of R, D, R, D, R, D, R, k3 TB k1 ***<br>....k9 (c s2kp c k7) 6 times, k2....k1, repeat *** — *** | (140)<br>+(71) +(140) |
| 65 | S1pw *** T k2, Row 1 of R, D, R, D, R, D, R, k2 TB k1 ***<br>....k3 (Tc k1 cTB k5) 6 times, Tc k1 cTB k3....k1, repeat *** — *** | (138)<br>+(71) +(138) |
| 67 | S1pw *** T k1, Row 3 of R, D, R, D, R, D, R, k1 TB k1 ***<br>....k2 (Tc k3 cTB k3) 6 times, Tc k3 cTB k2....k1, repeat *** — *** | (136)<br>+(71) +(136) |
| 69 | S1pw *** T, Row 5 of R, D, R, D, R, D, R, TB k1 ***<br>....k3 (cTB k1 Tc k5) 6 times, cTB k1 Tc k3....k1, repeat *** — *** | (134)<br>+(71) +(134) |
| 71 | S1pw *** T k3, c s2kp c k5, c s2kp c k4, Row 7 of D, R, D, R, D,<br>k4 c s2kp c k5 c s2kp c, k3 TB k1 ***<br>....k4 (c s2kp c k7) 6 times, c s2kp c k4....k1, repeat *** — *** | <br>(132)<br>+(71) +(132) |
| 73 | S1pw *** T k5, Tc k1 cTB k7, Row 9 of D, R, D, R, D, k7 Tc k1 cTB, k5 TB k1 ***<br>....k8 (Tc k1 cTB k5) 6 times, k3....k1, repeat *** — *** | (130)<br>+(71) +(130) |
| 75 | S1pw *** T k3, Tc k3 cTB k6, Row 11 of D, R, D, R, D, k6 Tc k3 cTB, k3 TB k1 ***<br>....k7 (Tc k3 cTB k3) 6 times, k4....k1, repeat *** — *** | (128)<br>+(71) +(128) |
| 77 | S1pw *** T k3, cTB k1 Tc k7, Row 13 of D, R, D, R, D, k7 cTB k1 Tc, k3 TB k1 ***<br>....k8 (cTB k1 Tc k5) 6 times, k3....k1, repeat *** — *** | (126)<br>+(71) +(126) |
| 79 | S1pw *** T k3, c s2kp c k8, Row 15 of D, R, D, R, D, k8 c s2kp c, k3 TB k1 ***<br>....k9 (c s2kp c k7) 6 times, k2....k1, repeat *** — *** | (124)<br>+(71) +(124) |

# *Cobweb Lace Wrap*

| ROW | | |
|---|---|---|
| 81 | S1pw *** T k5, Tc k1 cTB k3, Row 1 of D, R, D, R, D, k3 Tc k1 cTB, k5 TB k1 *** | (122) |
| | ....k3 (Tc k1 cTB k5) 6 times, Tc k1 cTB k3....k1, repeat *** — *** | +(71) +(122) |
| 83 | S1pw *** T k3, Tc k3 cTB k2, Row 3 of D, R, D, R, D, k2 Tc k3 cTB, k3 TB k1 *** | (120) |
| | ....k2 (Tc k3 cTB k3) 6 times, Tc k3 cTB k2....k1, repeat *** — *** | +(71) +(120) |
| 85 | S1pw *** T k3, cTB k1 Tc k3, Row 5 of D, R, D, R, D, k3 cTB k1 Tc, k3 TB k1 *** | (118) |
| | ....k3 (cTB k1 Tc k5) 6 times, cTB k1 Tc k3....k1, repeat *** — *** | +(71) +(118) |
| 87 | S1pw *** T k3, c s2kp c k4, Row 7 of D, R, D, R, D, k4 c s2kp c, k3 TB k1 *** | (116) |
| | ....k4 (c s2kp c k7) 6 times, c s2kp c k4....k1, repeat *** — *** | +(71) +(116) |
| 89 | S1pw *** T k9, Row 9 of D, R, D, R, D, k9 TB k1 *** | (114) |
| | ....k8 (Tc k1 cTB k5) 6 times, k3....k1, repeat *** — *** | +(71) +(114) |
| 91 | S1pw *** T k8, Row 11 of D, R, D, R, D, k8 TB k1 *** | (112) |
| | ....k7 (Tc k3 cTB k3) 6 times, k4....k1, repeat *** — *** | +(71) +(112) |
| 93 | S1pw *** T k7, Row 13 of D, R, D, R, D, k7 TB k1 *** | (110) |
| | ....k8 (cTB k1 Tc k5) 6 times, k3....k1, repeat *** — *** | +(71) +(110) |
| 95 | S1pw *** T k6, Row 15 of D, R, D, R, D, k6 TB k1 *** | (108) |
| | ....k9 (c s2kp c k7) 6 times, k2....k1, repeat *** — *** | +(71) +(108) |
| 97 | S1pw *** T k5, Row 1 of D, R, D, R, D, k5 TB k1 *** | (106) |
| | ....k3 (Tc k1 cTB k5) 6 times, Tc k1 cTB k3....k1, repeat *** — *** | +(71) +(106) |
| 99 | S1pw *** T k4, Row 3 of D, R, D, R, D, k4 TB k1 *** | (104) |
| | ....k2 (Tc k3 cTB k3) 6 times, Tc k3 cTB k2....k1, repeat *** — *** | +(71) +(104) |
| 101 | S1pw *** T k3, Row 5 of D, R, D, R, D, k3 TB k1 *** | (102) |
| | ....k3 (cTB k1 Tc k5) 6 times, cTB k1 Tc k3....k1, repeat *** — *** | +(71) +(102) |
| 103 | S1pw *** T k2, Row 7 of D, R, D, R, D, k2 TB k1 *** | (100) |
| | ....k4 (c s2kp c k7) 6 times, c s2kp c k4....k1, repeat *** — *** | +(71) +(100) |
| 105 | S1pw *** T k1, Row 9 of D, R, D, R, D, k1 TB k1 *** | (98) |
| | ....k8 (Tc k1 cTB k5) 6 times, k3....k1, repeat *** — *** | +(71) +(98) |
| 107 | S1pw *** T, Row 11 of D, R, D, R, D, TB k1 *** | (96) |
| | ....k7 (Tc k3 cTB k3) 6 times, k4....k1, repeat *** — *** | +(71) +(96) |
| 109 | S1pw *** T k3, cTB k2 c s2kp c k2 Tc k3, Row 13 of R, D, R, | |
| | k4 cTB k2 c s2kp c k2 Tc, k2 TB k1 *** | (94) |
| | ....k8 (cTB k1 Tc k5) 6 times, k3....k1, repeat *** — *** | +(71) +(94) |
| 111 | S1pw *** T k3, cTB k2 cTB k1 Tc k4, Row 15 of R, D, R, k5 cTB k2 cTB k1 Tc, k2 TB k1 *** | (92) |
| | ....k9 (c s2kp c k7) 6 times, k2....k1, repeat *** — *** | +(71) +(92) |

**ROW**

113 S1pw *** T k3, cTB k2 cTB k6, Row 1 of R, D, R, k6 cTB k2 cTB, k3 TB k1 *** (90)
....k3 (Tc k1 cTB k5) 6 times, Tc k1 cTB k3....k1, repeat *** — *** +(71) +(90)

115 S1pw *** T k3, cTB k2 cTB k5, Row 3 of R, D, R, k7 cTB k2 cTB, k1 TB k1 *** (88)
....k2 (Tc k3 cTB k3) 6 times, Tc k3 cTB k2....k1, repeat *** — *** +(71) +(88)

117 S1pw *** T k3, cTB k8, Row 5 of R, D, R, k8 cTB, k3 TB k1 *** (86)
....k3 (cTB k1 Tc k5) 6 times, cTB k1 Tc k3....k1, repeat *** — *** +(71) +(86)

119 S1pw *** T k3, cTB k7, Row 7 of R, D, R, k9 cTB, k1 TB k1 *** (84)
....k4 (c s2kp c k7) 6 times, c s2kp c k4....k1, repeat *** — *** +(71) +(84)

121 S1pw *** T k3 cTB k6, Row 9 of R, D, R, k10, c 3TB k1 *** (82)
....k8 (Tc k1 cTB k5) 6 times, k3....k1, repeat *** — *** +(71) +(82)

123 S1pw *** T k10, Row 11 of R, D, R, k10 TB k1 *** (80)
....k7 (Tc k3 cTB k3) 6 times, k4....k1, repeat *** — *** +(71) +(80)

125 S1pw *** T k9, Row 13 of R, D, R, k9 TB k1 *** (78)
....k8 (cTB k1 Tc k5) 6 times, k3....k1, repeat *** — *** +(71) +(78)

127 S1pw *** T k8, Row 15 of R, D, R, k8 TB k1 *** (76)
....k9 (c s2kp c k7) 6 times, k2....k1, repeat *** — *** +(71) +(76)

129 S1pw *** T k7, Row 1 of R, D, R, k7 TB k1 *** (74)
....k3 (Tc k1 cTB k5) 6 times, Tc k1 cTB k3....k1, repeat *** — *** +(71) +(74)

131 S1pw *** T k6, Row 3 of R, D, R, k6 TB k1 *** (72)
....k2 (Tc k3 cTB k3) 6 times, Tc k3 cTB k2....k1, repeat *** — *** +(71) +(72)

133 S1pw *** T k5, Row 5 of R, D, R, k5 TB k1 *** (70)
....k3 (cTB k1 Tc k5) 6 times, cTB k1 Tc k3....k1, repeat *** — *** +(71) +(70)

135 S1pw *** T k4, Row 7 of R, D, R, k4 TB k1 *** (68)
....k4 (c s2kp c k7) 6 times, c s2kp c k4....k1, repeat *** — *** +(71) +(68)

137 S1pw *** T k3, Row 9 of R, D, R, k3 TB k1 *** (66)
....k8 (Tc k1 cTB k5) 6 times, k3....k1, repeat *** — *** +(71) +(66)

139 S1pw *** T k2, Row 11 of R, D, R, k2 TB k1 *** (64)
....k7 (Tc k3 cTB k3) 6 times, k4....k1, repeat *** — *** +(71) +(64)

141 S1pw *** T k1, Row 13 of R, D, R, k1 TB k1 *** (62)
....k8 (cTB k1 Tc k5) 6 times, k3....k1, repeat *** — *** +(71) +(62)

143 S1pw *** T, Row 15 of R, D, R, TB k1 *** (60)
....k9 (c s2kp c k7) 6 times, k2....k1, repeat *** — *** +(71) +(60)

| ROW | | |
|---|---|---|
| 145 | S1pw *** T k10, Tc k1 cTB k3, Row 1 of D, k3 Tc k1 cTB, k10 TB k1 ***<br>....k3 (Tc k1 cTB k5) 6 times, Tc k1 cTB k3....k1, repeat *** — *** | (58)<br>+(71) +(58) |
| 147 | S1pw *** T k8, Tc k3 cTB k2, Row 3 of D, k2 Tc k3 cTB, k8 TB k1 ***<br>....k2 (Tc k3 cTB k3) 6 times, Tc k3 cTB k2....k1, repeat *** — *** | (56)<br>+(71) +(56) |
| 149 | S1pw *** T k8, cTB k1 Tc k3, Row 5 of D, k3 cTB k1 Tc, k8 TB k1 ***<br>....k3 (cTB k1 Tc k5) 6 times, cTB k1 Tc k3....k1, repeat *** — *** | (54)<br>+(71) +(54) |
| 151 | S1pw *** T k8, c s2kp c k4, Row 7 of D, k4 c s2kp c, k8 TB k1 ***<br>....k4 (c s2kp c k7) 6 times, c s2kp c k4....k1, repeat *** — *** | (52)<br>+(71) +(52) |
| 153 | S1pw *** T k14, Row 9 of D, k14 TB k1 ***<br>....k8 (Tc k1 cTB k5) 6 times, k3....k1, repeat *** — *** | (50)<br>+(71) +(50) |
| 155 | S1pw *** T k13, Row 11 of D, k13 TB k1 ***<br>....k7 (Tc k3 cTB k3) 6 times, k4....k1, repeat *** — *** | (48)<br>+(71) +(48) |
| 157 | S1pw *** T k12, Row 13 of D, k12 TB k1 ***<br>....k8 (cTB k1 Tc k5) 6 times, k3....k1, repeat *** — *** | (46)<br>+(71) +(46) |
| 159 | S1pw *** T k11, Row 15 of D, k11 TB k1 ***<br>....k9 (c s2kp c k7) 6 times, k2....k1, repeat *** — *** | (44)<br>+(71) +(44) |
| 161 | S1pw *** T k10, Row 1 of D, k10 TB k1 ***<br>....k3 (Tc k1 cTB k5) 6 times, Tc k1 cTB k3....k1, repeat *** — *** | (42)<br>+(71) +(42) |
| 163 | S1pw *** T k9, Row 3 of D, k9 TB k1 ***<br>....k2 (Tc k3 cTB k3) 6 times, Tc k3 cTB k2....k1, repeat *** — *** | (40)<br>+(71) +(40) |
| 165 | S1pw *** T k8, Row 5 of D, k8 TB k1 ***<br>....k3 (cTB k1 Tc k5) 6 times, cTB k1 Tc k3....k1, repeat *** — *** | (38)<br>+(71) +(38) |
| 167 | S1pw *** T k7, Row 7 of D, k7 TB k1 ***<br>....k4 (c s2kp c k7) 6 times, c s2kp c k4....k1, repeat *** — *** | (36)<br>+(71) +(36) |
| 169 | S1pw *** T k6, Row 9 of D, k6 TB k1 ***<br>....k8 (Tc k1 cTB k5) 6 times, k3....k1, repeat *** — *** | (34)<br>+(71) +(34) |
| 171 | S1pw *** T k5, Row 11 of D, k5 TB k1 ***<br>....k7 (Tc k3 cTB k3) 6 times, k4....k1, repeat *** — *** | (32)<br>+(71) +(32) |
| 173 | S1pw *** T k4, Row 13 of D, k4 TB k1 ***<br>....k8 (cTB k1 Tc k5) 6 times, k3....k1, repeat *** — *** | (30)<br>+(71) +(30) |
| 175 | S1pw *** T k3, Row 15 of D, k3 TB k1 ***<br>....k9 (c s2kp c k7) 6 times, k2....k1, repeat *** — *** | (28)<br>+(71) +(28) |

**ROW**

| | | |
|---|---|---|
| 177 | S1pw *** T k6, TB cTB k2, c s2kp c T, k5 TB k1 ***<br>....k3 (Tc k1 cTB k5) 6 times, Tc k1 cTB k3....k1, repeat *** — *** | (24)<br>+(71) +(24) |
| 179 | S1pw *** T k5, TB cTB k1 TB cTB, k4 TB k1 ***<br>....k2 (Tc k3 cTB k3) 6 times, Tc k3 cTB k2....k1, repeat *** — *** | (20)<br>+(71) +(20) |
| 181 | S1pw *** T k4, TB c s2kp c TB, k3 TB k1 ***<br>....k3 (cTB k1 Tc k5) 6 times, cTB k1 Tc k3....k1, repeat *** — *** | (16)<br>+(71) +(16) |
| 183 | S1pw *** T k3, TB k1 T, k2 TB k1 ***<br>....k4 (c s2kp c k7) 6 times, c s2kp c k4....k1, repeat *** — *** | (12)<br>+(71) +(12) |
| 185 | S1pw *** T k1, TB k1 T, TB k1 ***<br>....k8 (Tc k1 cTB k5) 6 times, k3....k1, repeat *** — *** | (8)<br>+(71) +(8) |
| 187 | S1pw *** T, TB, TB k1 *** ....k7 (Tc k3 cTB k3) 6 times, k4....k1, repeat *** — *** | (5) +(71) +(5) |
| 188 | Slip 1 knitwise, purl to end. | |

Break off wool, leaving sufficient to darn in after dressing the garment.

**EDGE FINISHING INSTRUCTIONS**

With right side of work facing, and using No.11 needle, rejoin wool at RIGHT-HAND side of the garment immediately above the stitches on the pin. Pick up and knit evenly the row-end stitches from the side panel, working the remaining centre panel stitches as follows :
K1 s2kp k1....k8 (cTB k1 Tc k5) 6 times, k3....k1 s2kp k1, and continue, picking up and knitting the LEFT-HAND side panel stitches. Check that you have picked up all of the side panel stitches which now require to be reduced to 177 stitches on each side in order to create a neat edge to the garment.

Next row — Purl (LEFT-HAND side), reducing to 177 sts. by taking 2 sts. together at even intervals,
purl 3....purl 71 (centre)....purl 3, and continue
Purl (RIGHT-HAND side), again reducing to 177 sts.
Take together the last stitch with the first stitch from the pin. **(Total of 431 sts.)**

**NOTE** : From now on the 'pin' stitches will be worked, one by one, with the last stitch of every row.

Next row — Knit 180 (RIGHT-HAND side)....k9 (c s2kp c k7) 6 times, k2....knit 180 (LEFT-HAND side).

Next row — Purl (from LEFT to RIGHT).

## *Cobweb Lace Wrap*

Work the following 24 row sequence of Roundel stitch.

1st Row K3 (Tc k1 cTB k5) 42 times, Tc k1 cTB k3

**2nd and every alternate row — purl.**

3rd Row K2 (Tc k3 cTB k3) 42 times, Tc k3 cTB k2

5th Row K3 (cTB k1 Tc k5) 42 times, cTB k1 Tc k3

7th Row K4 (c s2kp c k7) 42 times, c s2kp c k4

9th Row K8 (Tc k1 cTB k5) 41 times, Tc k1 cTB k8

11th Row K7 (Tc k3 cTB k3) 41 times, Tc k3 cTB k7

13th Row K8 (cTB k1 Tc k5) 41 times, cTB k1 Tc k8

15th Row K9 (c s2kp c k7) 41 times, c s2kp c k9

17th Row K3 (Tc k1 cTB k5) 42 times, Tc k1 cTB k3

19th Row K2 (Tc k3 cTB k3) 42 times, Tc k3 cTB k2

21st Row K3 (cTB k1 Tc k5) 42 times, cTB k1 Tc k3

23rd Row K4 (c s2kp c k7) 42 times, c s2kp c k4

24th Row Purl

Knit one further row, taking up the last 'pin' stitch from the LEFT-HAND side, and continue by picking up and knitting the 18 sts. from the 'cast-on' edge of the border lace scallops.

Next row — Purl 2 together, knit 16, Moss st. 431 to end (starting K1, P1), and continue by picking up and knitting the 18 sts. from the 'cast-off' edge of the RIGHT-HAND side scallops.

Next row — Knit 2 together, knit 16, Moss st. 431 (starting K1, P1), then knit 12, leaving the last 5 sts. on needle (LEFT-HAND side), **TURN** and continue,

Next row — Knit 12, Moss st. 431, knit 12, leaving the last 5 sts. on needle (RIGHT-HAND side).

Work a further 4 rows in Moss stitch, but keeping the scallop stitches in garter stitch, and leaving a further 5 sts. on needle at the end of each row. (Total of 15 sts. on needle at each side).

Next two rows — Moss stitch **WHOLE ROW** (including the 15 stitches held at each end).

**WITH No.10 NEEDLE, CAST OFF EVENLY, BUT NOT TIGHTLY**

**TO FINISH, SEW IN ENDS WHERE NECESSARY, CUTTING OFF ENDS AFTER DRESSING**

**TO DRESS WRAP** : Wash **BY HAND ONLY** in lukewarm soapy water, squeezing gently. Rinse in lukewarm water. Roll up in a towel to absorb excess moisture. Dry flat on a white sheet, away from heat or sun, pinning out to approximately 66″ along the straight edge, and 46″ on each side, ensuring that each point is pinned out. The length from the centre of the long edge to the centre of the double scallop should be approximately 36″.

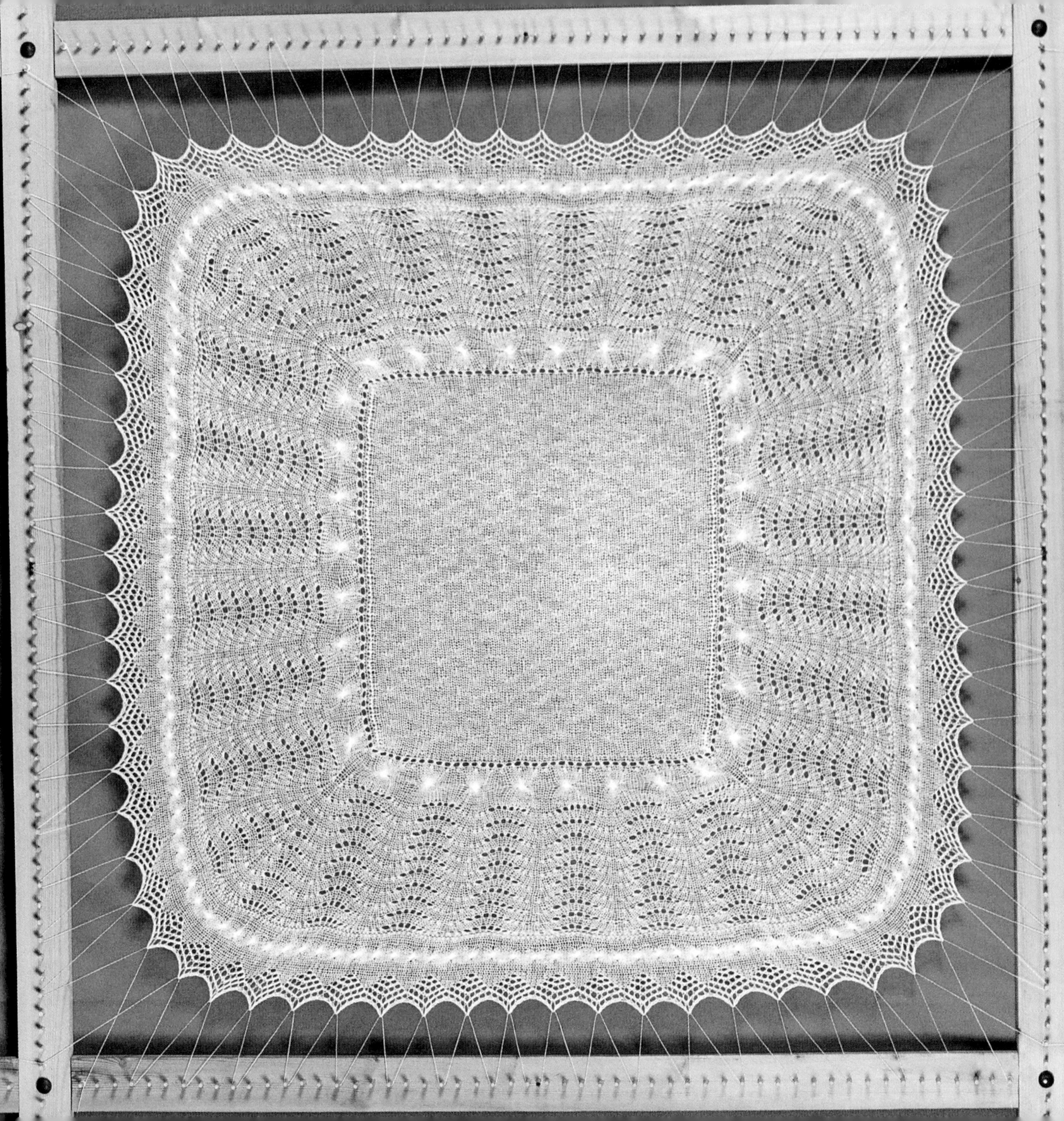

# *The Philip & Michael Shawl*

## A BABY SHAWL KNITTED IN 2-PLY LACE WOOL

### Size — 50'' x 50'' (125cm x 125cm)

**Materials** : 6 hanks 2-ply lace wool
1 circular needle — size 8 (4mm) — 30" (80cm) long
1 cable needle

A warm but light-weight baby shawl, the main border is worked on a circular needle in the round. The centre is then knitted from side to side in Basket stitch. An alternative centre pattern can be used.

*The Philip & Michael Shawl*

**NOTE.**

**SPECIAL ABBREVIATIONS :**
**CABLE '6'** — Slip next 3 sts. on to cable needle and hold in front; k3, then k3 from cable needle.
**CABLE '8'** — Slip next 4 sts. on to cable needle and hold in front; k4, then k4 from cable needle.

**BORDER LACE** : With No.8 needle cast on 23 stitches **VERY** loosely.

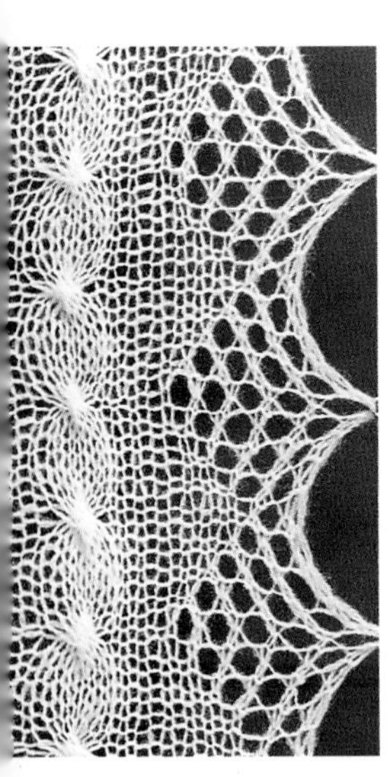

1st Row : S1pw k4 p6 k3................k9 (23)

2nd Row : S1pw TcT k4..................p3 CABLE'6' p3 k2 (22)

3rd Row : S1pw k4 p6 k3................k8 (22)

4th Row : S1pw k1 cTc k4...............p3 k6 p3 k2 (23)

5th Row : S1pw k4 p6 k3................k9 (23)

6th Row : S1pw k1 (cT) twice, c k3....p3 k6 p3 k2 (24)

7th Row : S1pw k4 p6 k3................k10 (24)

8th Row : S1pw k1 (cT) 3 times, c k2...p3 k6 p3 k2 (25)

9th Row : S1pw k4 p6 k3................k11 (25)

10th Row : S1pw k1 (cT) 4 times, c k1...p3 CABLE'6' p3 k2 (26)

11th Row : S1pw k4 p6 k3................k12 (26)

12th Row : S1pw (Tc) 4 times, T k1......p3 k6 p3 k2 (25)

13th Row : S1pw k4 p6 k3................k11 (25)

14th Row : S1pw (Tc) 3 times,T k2.......p3 k6 p3 k2 (24)

15th Row : S1pw k4 p6 k3................k10 (24)

16th Row : S1pw (Tc) twice, T k3........p3 k6 p3 k2 (23)

**These 16 rows form one scallop and two cable twists, which are worked continuously until 72 scallops have been completed.**

**Graft together cast-on stitches and stitches from last row of border lace.**

**NOTE : 72 scallops produce 576 sts. equalling 144 per side.**

**MAIN BORDER**

**From border lace with right side of work facing — pick up 576 stitches, and (knit 144 sts. through back loops) 4 times, putting in marker threads at the end of each 144 sts. (i.e. at the four corners).**

**NOTE** : The **'K1'** at the beginning of each pattern row is the corner stitch and is constant throughout the main border. From now on instructions are given for **ONE SIDE ONLY** to be worked **FOUR TIMES CONTINUOUSLY,** up to the cable sequence.

Knit one row. Purl one row.

1st pattern row : (K1 T T T (c k1) 5 times, c T T T) 8 times. (144)

Purl one row. Knit three rows. Purl one row.

2nd pattern row : (K1 T T T (c k1) 5 times, c T T T) 8 times. (144)

Purl one row. Knit three rows. Purl one row.

3rd pattern row : K1 3T T T (c k1) 4 times, c T T T,
(k1 T T T (c k1) 5 times, c T T T) 6 times, k1 T T T (c k1) 4 times, c T T 3T (140)

Purl one row. Knit three rows. Purl one row.

4th pattern row : K1 3T T k1 (c k1) 3 times, c T T T,
(k1 T T T (c k1) 5 times, c T T T) 6 times, k1 T T T (c k1) 3 times, c k1 T 3T (136)

Purl one row. Knit three rows. Purl one row.

5th pattern row : K1 3T T (c k1) twice, c T T T,
(k1 T T T (c k1) 5 times, c T T T) 6 times, k1 T T T (c k1) twice, c T 3T (130)

Purl one row. Knit three rows. Purl one row.

6th pattern row : K1 3T c k1 c T T T,
(k1 T T T (c k1) 5 times, c T T T) 6 times, k1 T T T c k1 c 3T (124)

Purl one row. Knit three rows. Purl one row.

7th pattern row : K1 3T c T T (k1 T T T (c k1) 5 times, c T T T) 6 times, k1 T T c 3T (118)

Purl one row. Knit three rows. Purl one row.

8th pattern row : K1 T T (k1 T T T (c k1) 5 times, c T T T) 6 times, k1 T T (114)

Purl one row. Knit three rows. Purl one row.

9th pattern row : K1 3T T T T (c k1) 5 times, c T T T,
(k1 T T T (c k1) 5 times, c T T T) 5 times, 3T (110)

Purl one row. Knit three rows. Purl one row.

10th pattern row : K1 3T T T (c k1) 5 times, c T T T,
(k1 T T T (c k1) 5 times, c T T T) 4 times, k1 T T T (c k1) 5 times, c T T 3T (108)

Purl one row.

Next row — K1 T, knit 103, T (106)

Next row — Knit all round.

Next row — K1 T, knit 101, T (104)

**CABLE SEQUENCE**

**NOTE** : The original corner stitch will become the centre stitch of a purl 5 set of sts. in the cable sequence, and the **TOTAL** stitch count for the round is now shown.

**Knit 3 stitches,** then work as follows :

1st cable row : (k8 p5) 32 times. (416)

Repeat 1st cable row a further 5 times.

2nd cable row : (CABLE '8' p5) 32 times. (416)

Repeat 1st cable row a further 5 times.

3rd cable row : (k8 p5) 31 times, k8 (411 sts.), then continue,

4th cable row : (T k1 T, k3 T k3) 32 times. (320)

5th cable row : purl all round. (320)

6th cable row : (cT) 160 times. (320 sts., 4 sides of 80 sts.)

Purl one row. Knit one row.

**NOTE** : From now on the shawl is worked over 80 stitches starting from one side, and working up to the opposite side, taking together the last stitch of each row with one stitch from the left and right sides alternately, until all of the stitches from these sides have been used up — 160 rows in all. The stitches from the last side are then grafted to the worked centre.

A choice of **EITHER** a Basket stitch or Double Moss stitch centre pattern has been given, knit the one you prefer or a centre of your own design.

**BASKET STITCH CENTRE**

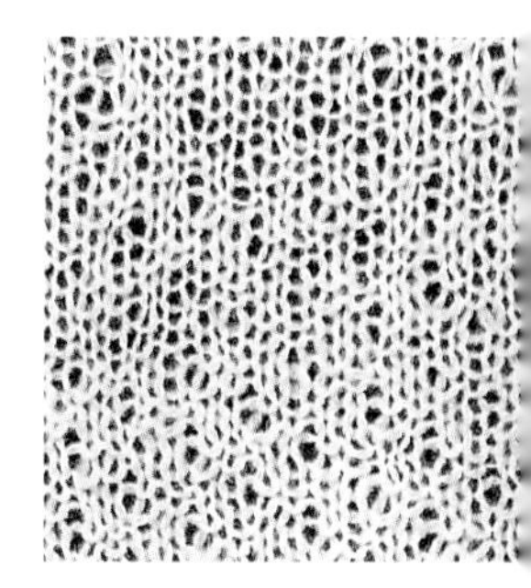

1st Basket row : On the first 80 stitches, work (k4 p4) to end, taking up one stitch from the side with the last purl stitch.

Repeat 1st Basket row a further 3 times.

2nd Basket row : Work (p4 k4) to end, taking up one stitch from the side with the last knit stitch.

Repeat 2nd Basket row a further 3 times.

Continue, repeating the above 8 row sequence until the 80 stitches from the left and right side are used up, (160 rows), leaving 80 sts. on the remaining side to be grafted to the worked centre.

Alternative **DOUBLE MOSS STITCH CENTRE**

1st Moss row : On the first 80 stitches, work (k2 p2) to end, taking up one stitch from the side with the last purl stitch.

Repeat 1st Moss row once.

2nd Moss row : Work (p2 k2) to end, taking up one stitch from the side with the last knit stitch.

Repeat 2nd Moss row once.

Continue, repeating the above 4 row sequence until the 80 stitches from the left and right side are used up, (160 rows), leaving 80 sts. on the remaining side to be grafted to the worked centre.

**TO DRESS SHAWL** : Wash **BY HAND ONLY** in lukewarm soapy water, squeezing gently. Rinse in lukewarm water. Roll up in a towel to absorb excess moisture. Stretch out to dry to a perfect square 50" x 50" approx., away from heat or sun, on a shawl frame or pin out scallops at points on to a white sheet, and dry flat.

# *Circular Shaded Shawl*

## KNITTED IN 2-PLY LACE WOOL

### Size — 52'' diameter (130cm)

**MATERIALS** : 1 hank each of the following shades in 2-ply lace wool :
2oz. hank — SHETLAND BLACK — L5
2oz. hank — MOORIT — L4
1oz. hank — DARK NATURAL — L78
1oz. hank — MEDIUM NATURAL — L3
1oz. hank — LIGHT NATURAL — L202
1oz. hank — WHITE (NATURAL) — L1a

1 circular needle — size 7 (4.50mm) — 30'' (80cm) long
1 circular needle — size 7 (4.50mm) — 24'' (60cm) long
4 double-ended needles — size 8 (4.00mm)
4 double-ended needles — size 9 (3.75mm)

This version of Old Shale stitch has been slightly updated to produce a fashion garment more suitable for present-day use. It still has fine warm properties and is an extremely useful accessory.

The colours used in this pattern are natural ones, but should the knitter wish to use a different colour range it should be noted that if less than six colours are used the quantity of each one will need to be adjusted.

The main part of the shawl is knitted on the 30'' No.7 circular needle. Towards the centre it will be necessary to change to the 24'' needle in order not to stretch the work unduly. After the 24th pattern row the work is continued on the 4 double-ended, No.8 needles.

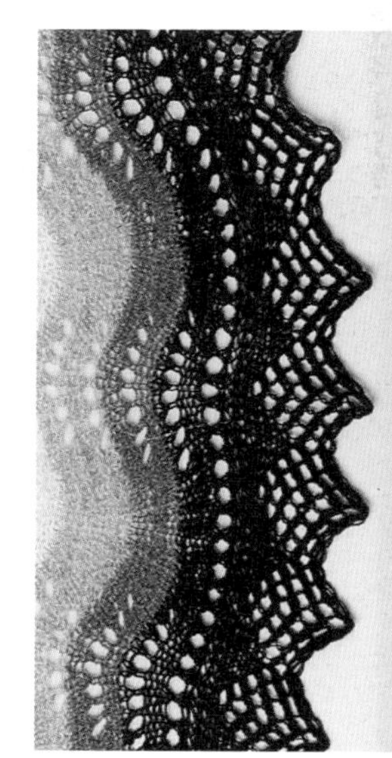

**BORDER LACE** : With No.7 needle, and **SHADE L5** cast on 10 stitches **VERY** loosely.

1st Row : S1pw k1 cTc, k6 (11)

**2nd and every alternate row : S1pw knit to end.**

3rd Row : S1pw k1 (cT) twice, c k5 (12)

5th Row : S1pw k1 (cT) 3 times, c k4 (13)

7th Row : S1pw k1 (cT) 4 times, c k3 (14)

9th Row : S1pw T (cT) 4 times, k3 (13)

11th Row : S1pw T (cT) 3 times, k4 (12)

13th Row : S1pw T (cT) twice, k5 (11)

15th Row : S1pw TcT, k6 (10)

16th Row : S1pw knit to end.

**These 16 rows form one scallop,** and are worked continuously until 72 scallops have been completed. Graft together the cast-on stitches and the stitches from the last row of the border lace.

**NOTE** : 72 scallops produce 576 stitches.

# *The Belinda Skirt*

### KNITTED IN 2-PLY LACE WOOL

### Size — To fit up to 44'' (112cm) hip

**MATERIALS** : 1oz. hanks of the following shades in 2-ply lace wool :
4 hanks — ROYAL BLUE — L18 (main colour)
2 hanks — MEDIUM BLUE — L16
2 hanks — LIGHT BLUE — L15
2 hanks — VERY LIGHT BLUE — L14
2 hanks — WHITE — L1
1" elastic for waistband
1 circular needle — size 7 (4.50mm) — 30" (80cm) long
1 circular needle — size 7 (4.50mm) — 24" (60cm) long
1 circular needle — size 9 (3.75mm) — 24" (60cm) long

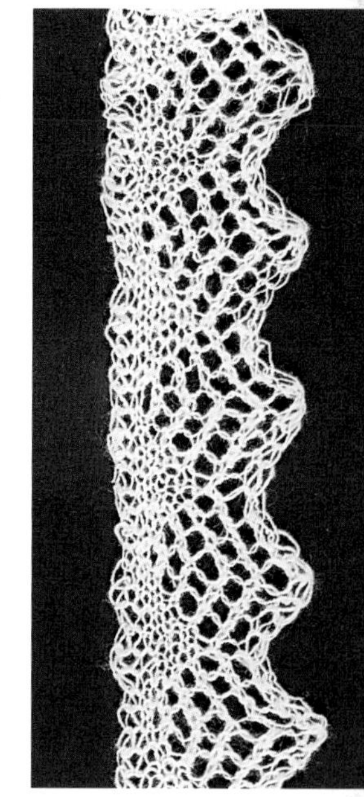

This pattern, for a circular skirt knitted in Old Shale stitch, can be produced in any colourway desired. The original is knitted in shades of blue, from deep royal, through dark, medium and light blue to white. Materials and instructions are given for this version. If other colours are used, it is important to note where colour changes occur, and these should never be before a purl row. The waist is elasticated to suit. The pattern will produce a skirt of approximately 30" in length. If a shorter length is required, this can be achieved by working only to pattern row 23, before knitting the waistband, or alternatively by starting the Old Shale from pattern row 5, which will mean that only 78 scallops will be required, and the pick-up will be 624 stitches.

The main body of the skirt is knitted on the 30" No.7 circular needle. Towards the waistband it will be necessary to change to the 24" needle in order not to stretch the work unduly, and the waistband is knitted on the No.9 needle.

**BORDER LACE** : With No.7 needle, and **SHADE L18** cast on 10 stitches **VERY** loosely.

1st Row : S1pw k1 cTc, k6 (11)

**2nd and every alternate row : S1pw knit to end.**

3rd Row : S1pw k1 (cT) twice, c k5 (12)

5th Row : S1pw k1 (cT) 3 times, c k4 (13)

7th Row : S1pw k1 (cT) 4 times, c k3 (14)

9th Row : S1pw T (cT) 4 times, k3 (13)

11th Row : S1pw T (cT) 3 times, k4 (12)

13th Row : S1pw T (cT) twice, k5 (11)

15th Row : S1pw TcT, k6 (10)

16th Row : S1pw knit to end.

**These 16 rows form one scallop,** and are worked continuously until 90 scallops have been completed. Graft together the cast-on stitches and the stitches from the last row of the border lace.

**NOTE** : 90 scallops produce 720 stitches.

# *The Belinda Skirt*

**NOTE** : The six row Old Shale stitch pattern is worked — purl row, pattern row, purl row, and three knit rows — the purl rows always being either side of the pattern row and therefore emphasising the pattern row. The sequence is maintained throughout.

**From border lace — pick up 720 stitches, from the straight edge, and knit one row through back loops. Put in a marker thread at the end of the round.**

Purl one row. (720)

Next row — (cT) all round (360 times) (720)

Purl one row. Knit three rows. Purl one row.

1st pattern row : (K1 T T T T T (c k1) 9 times, c T T T T T) 24 times. (720)

Purl one row. **COLOUR CHANGE L16** Knit three rows. Purl one row.

2nd pattern row : (K1 T T T T T (c k1) 9 times, c T T T T T) 24 times. (720)

Purl one row. Knit two rows. **COLOUR CHANGE L15** Knit one row. Purl one row.

3rd pattern row : (K1 T T T T T (c k1) 9 times, c T T T T T) 24 times. (720)

Purl one row. Knit three rows. Purl one row.

**COLOUR CHANGE L14**

4th pattern row : (K1 T T T T T (c k1) 9 times, c T T T T T) 24 times. (720)

Purl one row. Knit three rows. Purl one row.

**COLOUR CHANGE L1**

5th pattern row : (K1 T T T T 3T (c k1) 7 times, c 3T T T T T) 24 times. (624)

Purl one row. Knit three rows. Purl one row.

**COLOUR CHANGE L18**

6th pattern row : (K1 T T T T k1 (c k1) 7 times, c k1 T T T T) 24 times. (624)

Purl one row. Knit three rows. Purl one row.

7th pattern row : (K1 T T T T k1 (c k1) 7 times, c k1 T T T T) 24 times. (624)

Purl one row. Knit two rows. **COLOUR CHANGE L16** Knit one row. Purl one row.

8th pattern row : (K1 T T T T k1 (c k1) 7 times, c k1 T T T T) 24 times. (624)

Purl one row. Knit three rows. Purl one row.

**COLOUR CHANGE L15**

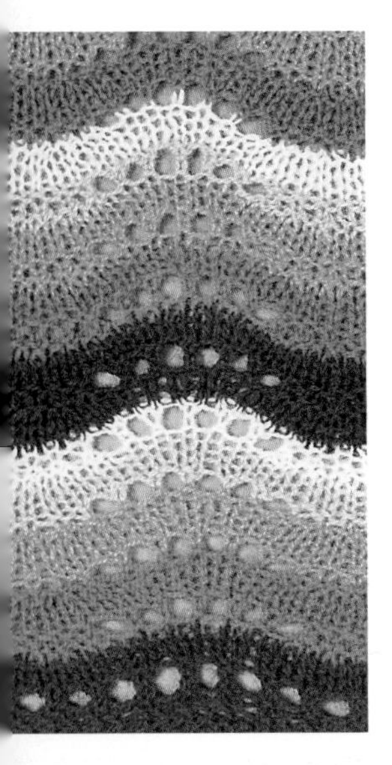

9th pattern row : (K1 3T T T T (c k1) 7 times, c T T T 3T) 24 times. (576)

Purl one row. Knit three rows. Purl one row.

10th pattern row : (K1 T T T T (c k1) 7 times, c T T T T) 24 times. (576)

Purl one row. **COLOUR CHANGE L14** Knit three rows. Purl one row.

11th pattern row : (K1 T T T T (c k1) 7 times, c T T T T) 24 times. (576)

Purl one row. **COLOUR CHANGE L1** Knit three rows. Purl one row.

12th pattern row : (K1 3T T T T (c k1) 5 times, c T T T 3T) 24 times. (480)

Purl one row. **COLOUR CHANGE L18** Knit three rows. Purl one row.

13th pattern row : (K1 T T T T (c k1) 5 times, c T T T T) 24 times. (480)

Purl one row. Knit two rows. **COLOUR CHANGE L16** Knit one row. Purl one row.

14th pattern row : (K1 T T T T (c k1) 5 times, c T T T T) 24 times. (480)

Purl one row. Knit three rows. Purl one row.

**COLOUR CHANGE L15**

15th pattern row : (K1 3T T T (c k1) 5 times, c T T 3T) 24 times. (432)

Purl one row. Knit three rows. Purl one row.

16th pattern row : (K1 T T T (c k1) 5 times, c T T T) 24 times. (432)

Purl one row. **COLOUR CHANGE L14** Knit three rows. Purl one row.

17th pattern row : (K1 T T T (c k1) 5 times, c T T T) 24 times. (432)

Purl one row. **COLOUR CHANGE L1** Knit three rows. Purl one row.

18th pattern row : (K1 3T T T (c k1) 3 times, c T T 3T) 24 times. (336)

Purl one row. **COLOUR CHANGE L16** Knit three rows. Purl one row.

19th pattern row : (K1 T T k1 (c k1) 3 times, c k1 T T) 24 times. (336)

Purl one row. Knit two rows. **COLOUR CHANGE L15** Knit one row. Purl one row.

20th pattern row : (K1 T T k1 (c k1) 3 times, c k1 T T) 24 times. (336)

Purl one row. Knit two rows. **COLOUR CHANGE L14** Knit one row. Purl one row.

21st pattern row : (K1 3T T (c k1) 3 times, c T 3T) 24 times. (288)

**CHANGE TO 24" NEEDLE**

Purl one row. Knit two rows. **COLOUR CHANGE L1** Knit one row. Purl one row.

*The Belinda Skirt*

22nd pattern row : (K1 T T (c k1) 3 times, c T T) 24 times. (288)

Purl one row. **COLOUR CHANGE L16** Knit three rows. Purl one row.

23rd pattern row : (K1 T T (c k1) 3 times, c T T) 24 times. (288)

Purl one row. Knit two rows. **COLOUR CHANGE L15** Knit one row. Purl one row.

24th pattern row : (K1 3T T c k1 c T 3T) 24 times. (192)

Purl one row. Knit two rows. **COLOUR CHANGE L14** Knit one row. Purl one row.

25th pattern row : (K1 T k1 c k1 c k1 T) 24 times. (192)

Purl one row. Knit two rows. **COLOUR CHANGE L1** Knit one row. Purl one row.

26th pattern row : (K1 T k1 c k1 c k1 T) 24 times. (192)

Purl one row. **COLOUR CHANGE L15** Knit three rows. Purl one row.

27th pattern row : (K1 T k1 c k1 c k1 T) 24 times. (192)

Purl one row. **COLOUR CHANGE L14**

**CHANGE TO No.9 NEEDLE**

Knit 25 rows, (for waistband). (192)

**CAST OFF VERY LOOSELY USING No.7 NEEDLE**

Fold waistband in half to inside, and stitch in place leaving 2″ open to allow threading of elastic.

**DARN IN ENDS, AND CUT OFF AFTER DRESSING**

**TO DRESS SKIRT** : Wash **BY HAND ONLY** in lukewarm soapy water, squeezing gently. Rinse in lukewarm water. Roll up in a towel to absorb excess moisture. Stretch out to shape, to dry away from heat or sun, on a white sheet and dry flat. Thread elastic into waist.

# *The Belinda Cape*

## KNITTED IN 2-PLY LACE WOOL

**Size — Length 24'' (60 cm) (To fit adult)**

**MATERIALS** : 1oz. hanks of the following shades in 2-ply lace wool :
2 hanks — ROYAL BLUE — L18 (main colour)
1 hank — MEDIUM BLUE — L16
1 hank — LIGHT BLUE — L15
1 hank — VERY LIGHT BLUE — L14
1 hank — WHITE — L1
2 buttons of your choice
1 circular needle — size 7 (4.50mm) — 24'' (60cm) long
1 circular needle — size 9 (3.75mm) — 16'' (40cm) long

This pattern, for a circular cape knitted in Old Shale stitch, can be produced in any colourway desired. The original is knitted in shades of blue, from deep royal, through dark, medium and light blue to white, and is a useful accessory to the Belinda skirt. Materials and instructions are given for this version. If other colours are used, it is important to note where colour changes occur.

The main part of the cape is knitted on the 24'' No.7 circular needle. The neckband is knitted on the No.9 needle.

**BORDER LACE** : With No.7 needle, and **SHADE L18** cast on 11 stitches **VERY** loosely.

Starter row — S1pw TcT, k6 (10)
Next row — S1pw knit to end.
**KNIT THESE TWO ROWS BEFORE THE FIRST SCALLOP ONLY**

1st Row : S1pw k1 cTc, k6 (11)

**2nd and every alternate row : S1pw knit to end.**

3rd Row : S1pw k1 (cT) twice, c k5 (12)

5th Row : S1pw k1 (cT) 3 times, c k4 (13)

7th Row : S1pw k1 (cT) 4 times, c k3 (14)

9th Row : S1pw T (cT) 4 times, k3 (13)

11th Row : S1pw T (cT) 3 times, k4 (12)

13th Row : S1pw T (cT) twice, k5 (11)

15th Row : S1pw TcT, k6 (10)

16th Row : S1pw knit to end.

**These 16 rows form one scallop,** and are worked continuously until 60 scallops have been completed, then CAST OFF.

**NOTE** : 60 scallops produce 480 stitches.

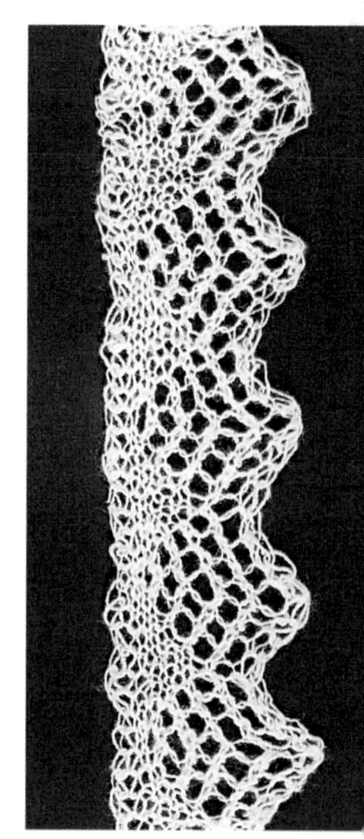

# *The Belinda Cape*

**NOTE** : The six row Old Shale stitch pattern is worked — pattern row, two knit rows, purl row and two knit rows. To emphasise the pattern row the knit rows, worked from the opposite side of the cape, are used before and after the pattern row, and colours should not be changed before working these rows. The sequence is maintained throughout.

**From Border Lace — Starting at RIGHT-HAND side, pick up 480 stitches from the straight edge, and Knit one row through back loops.**

Purl one row. Knit one row. Purl one row. Knit two rows.

1st pattern row : (K1 T T T T (c k1) 7 times, c T T T T) 20 times. (480)

Knit two rows. Purl one row. Knit two rows.

2nd pattern row : (K1 T T T T (c k1) 7 times, c T T T T) 20 times. (480)

Knit one row. **COLOUR CHANGE L16**

Knit one row. Purl one row. Knit two rows.

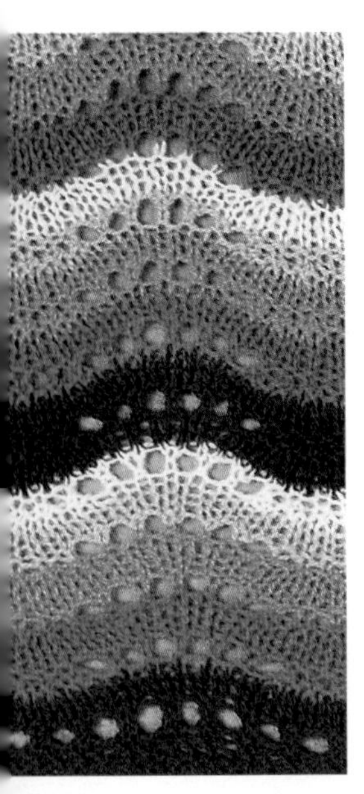

3rd pattern row : (K1 3T T T T (c k1) 5 times, c T T T 3T) 20 times. (400)

Knit two rows. Purl one row. Knit two rows. **COLOUR CHANGE L15**

4th pattern row : (K1 T T T k1 (c k1) 5 times, c k1 T T T) 20 times. (400)

Knit two rows. Purl one row. Knit two rows.

5th pattern row : (K1 T T T k1 (c k1) 5 times, c k1 T T T) 20 times. (400)

Knit one row. **COLOUR CHANGE L14**

Knit one row. Purl one row. Knit two rows.

6th pattern row : (K1 T T T k1 (c k1) 5 times, c k1 T T T) 20 times. (400)

Knit one row. **COLOUR CHANGE L1**

Knit one row. Purl one row. Knit two rows. **COLOUR CHANGE L18**

7th pattern row : (K1 3T T T (c k1) 5 times, c T T 3T) 20 times. (360)

Knit two rows. Purl one row. Knit two rows.

8th pattern row : (K1 T T T (c k1) 5 times, c T T T) 20 times. (360)

Knit one row. **COLOUR CHANGE L16**

Knit one row. Purl one row. Knit two rows.

9th pattern row : (K1 T T T (c k1) 5 times, c T T T) 20 times. (360)

Knit one row. **COLOUR CHANGE L15**

Knit one row. Purl one row. Knit two rows.

10th pattern row : (K1 T T T (c k1) 5 times, c T T T) 20 times. (360)

Knit one row. **COLOUR CHANGE L14**

Knit one row. Purl one row. Knit two rows.

11th pattern row : (K1 3T T T (c k1) 3 times, c T T 3T) 20 times. (280)

Knit one row. **COLOUR CHANGE L1**

Knit one row. Purl one row. Knit two rows.**COLOUR CHANGE L18**

12th pattern row : (K1 T T k1 (c k1) 3 times, c k1 T T) 20 times. (280)

Knit two rows. Purl one row. Knit two rows.

13th pattern row : (K1 T T k1 (c k1) 3 times, c k1 T T) 20 times. (280)

Knit one row. **COLOUR CHANGE L16**

Knit one row. Purl one row. Knit two rows.

14th pattern row : (K1 3T T (c k1) 3 times, c T 3T) 20 times. (240)

Knit one row. **COLOUR CHANGE L15**

Knit one row. Purl one row. Knit two rows.

15th pattern row : (K1 T T (c k1) 3 times, c T T) 20 times. (240)

Knit one row. **COLOUR CHANGE L14**

Knit one row. Purl one row. Knit two rows.

16th pattern row : (K1 T T (c k1) 3 times, c T T) 20 times. (240)

Knit one row. **COLOUR CHANGE L1**

Knit one row. Purl one row. Knit two rows. **COLOUR CHANGE L16**

17th pattern row : (K1 3T T c k1 c T 3T) 20 times. (160)

Knit two rows. Purl one row. Knit two rows. **COLOUR CHANGE L15**

18th pattern row : (K1 T k1 c k1 c k1 T) 20 times. (160)

Knit two rows. Purl one row. Knit two rows. **COLOUR CHANGE L14**

19th pattern row : (K1 T k1 c k1 c k1 T) 20 times. (160)

Knit two rows. Purl one row. **COLOUR CHANGE L1** Knit two rows.

20th pattern row : (K1 T k1 c k1 c k1 T) 20 times. (160)

Knit one row. **COLOUR CHANGE L15**

Knit one row. Purl one row. Knit two rows.

21st pattern row : (K1 3T c k1 c 3T) 20 times. (120)

Knit one row. **COLOUR CHANGE L14**

Knit one row. Purl one row. Knit two rows. **COLOUR CHANGE L1**

22nd pattern row : (K1 T c k1 c T) 20 times. (120)

Knit two rows. Purl one row. **COLOUR CHANGE L14** Knit two rows.

23rd pattern row : (K1 T c k1 c T) 20 times. (120)

Knit one row. **COLOUR CHANGE L1**

Knit one row. Purl one row. (120)

Leave the 120 stitches on a spare needle and proceed as follows :

**RIGHT FRONT** : With right side of work facing, and using No.7 needle and **SHADE L18,** pick up and knit cast-off stitches from RIGHT-HAND front border lace scallop, and continue, picking up and knitting the first stitch from every 2nd row end of the RIGHT-HAND side, to the neck edge. (82)

Next row — Knit 82 (finishing at scallop end).

1st pattern Row : K8 (k1 T T T (c k1) 5 times, c T T T) 4 times, k2 (82)

Knit three rows.

2nd pattern Row : Cast off 3 sts., K5 (k1 T T T (c k1) 5 times, c T T T) 4 times, k2 (79)

Knit three rows.

3rd pattern Row : Cast off 3 sts., K2 (k1 T T T (c k1) 5 times, c T T T) 4 times, k2 (76)

Knit one row.

Purl one row.

Cast off LOOSELY.

Continue with LEFT FRONT.

**LEFT FRONT** : With right side of work facing, and using No.7 needle and **SHADE L18,** start at neck edge and pick up and knit the first stitch from every 2nd row end of the LEFT-HAND side and cast-on stitches from LEFT-HAND front border scallop to match the opposite side (82)

Next row — Knit 82 (finishing at neck end).

1st pattern Row : K1 (k1 T T T (c k1) 5 times, c T T T) 4 times, k9 (82)

Knit two rows. Next row : Cast off 3 sts. k79 (to end) (79)

2nd pattern Row : K1 (k1 T T T (c k1) 5 times, c T T T) 4 times, k6

Knit two rows. Next row : Cast off 3 sts. k76 (to end) (76)

3rd pattern Row : K1 (k1 T T T (c k1) 5 times, c T T T) 4 times, k3

Knit one row.

Purl one row.

Cast off LOOSELY.

**NECKBAND** : With right side of work facing, and using No.9 needle and **SHADE L18,** pick up and knit 7 sts. from the RIGHT-HAND front edge, then across the 120 neck sts. taking together every 2nd. and 3rd. stitch i.e. (K1 T) 40 times, then pick up and knit the 7 sts. from the LEFT-HAND front edge.**(Total 94 sts.)**

Knit one row.

1st pattern Row : K3, cT (for buttonhole), k6 (k1 T T T (c k1) 5 times, c T T T) 4 times, k11 (94)

Knit three rows.

2nd pattern Row : K3, cT (for buttonhole), k6 (k1 T T T (c k1) 5 times, c T T T) 4 times, k11 (94)

Knit three rows.

Cast off with No.7 needle.

**DARN IN ENDS, AND CUT OFF AFTER DRESSING**

**TO DRESS CAPE** : Wash **BY HAND ONLY** in lukewarm soapy water, squeezing gently. Rinse in lukewarm water. Roll up in a towel to absorb excess moisture. Stretch out to dry to shape, away from heat or sun, and pin out scallops at points on to a white sheet, and dry flat.

Sew on buttons opposite buttonholes.

# *The Belinda Shoulder Shawl*

**KNITTED IN 2-PLY LACE WOOL**

**Size — 35'' x 35'' x 61'' (90 cm x 90 cm x 155 cm)**

**MATERIALS** : 1oz. hanks of the following shades in 2-ply lace wool :
2 hanks — ROYAL BLUE — L18 (main colour)
1 hank — MEDIUM BLUE — L16
1 hank — LIGHT BLUE — L15
1 hank — VERY LIGHT BLUE — L14
1 hank — WHITE — L1
1 circular needle — size 7 (4.50mm) — 24" (60cm) long

**The pattern can also be used for working with cobweb lace wool (3 hanks, using a No. 9 needle). This produces a fine shoulder wrap for a young bridesmaid. (Size, after dressing — 27" x 27" x 45")**

This shoulder shawl offers an alternative to the Belinda cape. It is a useful garment giving warmth to the shoulders without bulk or weight. The original was worked in the same colour range as the Belinda skirt and cape but many other attractive colourways may be used. It makes an ideal 'comforter' for chilly evenings.

**BORDER LACE** : With No.7 needle, and **SHADE L18** cast on 11 stitches **VERY** loosely.

Knit two rows.

Starter row — S1pw TcT, k6 (10)
Next row — S1pw knit to end.

**KNIT THESE FOUR ROWS BEFORE THE FIRST SCALLOP ONLY**

1st Row : S1pw k1 cTc, k6 (11)

**2nd and every alternate row : S1pw knit to end.**

3rd Row : S1pw k1 (cT) twice, c k5 (12)

5th Row : S1pw k1 (cT) 3 times, c k4 (13)

7th Row : S1pw k1 (cT) 4 times, c k3 (14)

9th Row : S1pw T (cT) 4 times, k3 (13)

11th Row : S1pw T (cT) 3 times, k4 (12)

13th Row : S1pw T (cT) twice, k5 (11)

15th Row : S1pw TcT, k6 (10)

16th Row : S1pw knit to end.

**These 16 rows form one scallop,** and are worked continuously until 39 scallops have been completed.

Knit a further two rows.

Cast off.

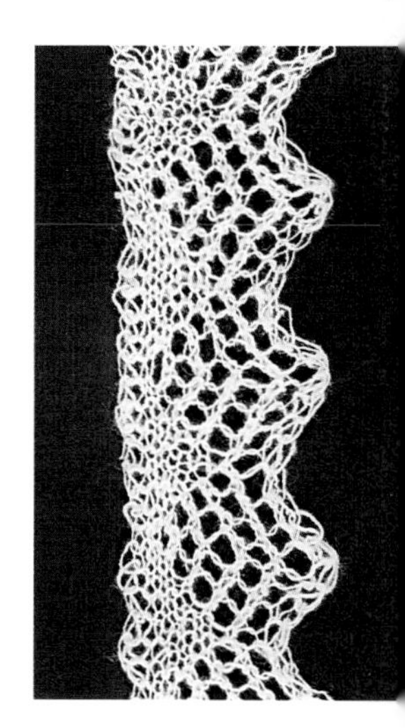

# *The Belinda Shoulder Shawl*

**From border lace — Starting at RIGHT-HAND side, pick up 315 stitches from the straight edge, and knit one row through back loops.**

Knit one row.

Pattern row — K1 (cT) to end.

Knit one row.

Knit a further row, **leaving first and last 11 sts. on safety pins for finishing off.**

Purl one row. **COLOUR CHANGE L16**

Decrease row — T, knit to last two sts. TB

Knit one row, **placing a coloured marker thread on the CENTRE STITCH.** (291)

**NOTE** : The six row Old Shale stitch pattern is worked as below, and to emphasise the pattern row the knit rows, worked from the opposite side of the shawl, are used before and after the pattern row, and colours should not be changed before working these rows.
The six row sequence is maintained throughout, as follows :
Pattern row (fully detailed).
Knit row.
Decrease row — T first two sts., Knit to two sts. **BEFORE** centre stitch — TB, k1 (centre stitch), T (two sts. **AFTER** centre stitch), knit to last two sts., TB
Purl row.
Decrease row — (as above decrease row).
Knit row.

1st pattern row : *** 3T T T (c k1) 5 times, c T T T (k1 T T T (c k1) 5 times, c T T T) 6 times, k1 T T T (c k1) 5 times, c T T 3TB *** , k1 (centre st.), repeat *** — *** (287)

Knit one row. Decrease row. Purl one row. Decrease row. Knit one row.

**COLOUR CHANGE L15**

2nd pattern row : *** T k2 (c k1) 5 times, c T T T (k1 T T T (c k1) 5 times, c T T T) 6 times, k1 T T T (c k1) 5 times, c k2 TB *** , k1 (centre st.), repeat *** — *** (287)

Knit one row. Decrease row. Purl one row. Decrease row. Knit one row.

**COLOUR CHANGE L14**

3rd pattern row : *** 3T T (c k1) 4 times, c T T T (k1 T T T (c k1) 5 times, c T T T) 6 times, k1 T T T (c k1) 4 times, c T 3TB *** , k1 (centre st.), repeat *** — *** (275)

Knit one row. Decrease row. Purl one row. **COLOUR CHANGE L1**

Decrease row. Knit one row.

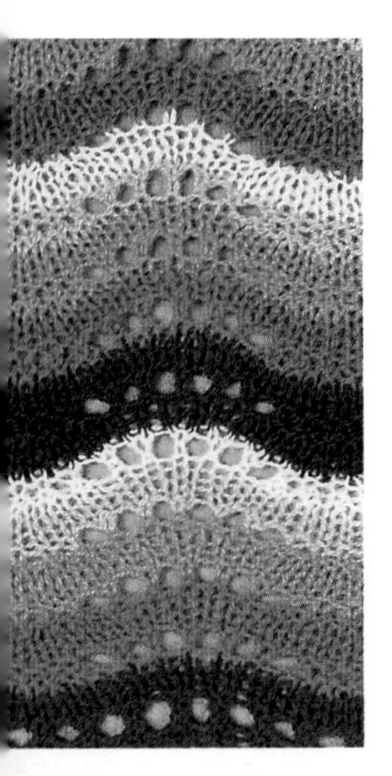

4th pattern row : *** T k1 (c k1) 3 times, c T T T (k1 T T T (c k1) 5 times, c T T T) 6 times, k1 T T T (c k1) 3 times, c k1 TB *** , k1 (centre st.), repeat *** — *** (267)

Knit one row. **COLOUR CHANGE L18**

Decrease row. Purl one row. Decrease row. Knit one row.

5th pattern row : *** T (c k1) twice, c T T T (k1 T T T (c k1) 5 times, c T T T) 6 times, k1 T T T (c k1) twice, c TB *** , k1 (centre st.), repeat *** — *** (255)

Knit one row. Decrease row. Purl one row. **COLOUR CHANGE L16**

Decrease row. Knit one row.

6th pattern row : *** T c k1 c T T (k1 T T T (c k1) 5 times, c T T T) 6 times, k1 T T c k1 c TB *** , k1 (centre st.), repeat *** — *** (243)

Knit one row. Decrease row. Purl one row. Decrease row. Knit one row.

**COLOUR CHANGE L15**

7th pattern row : *** T T (k1 T T T (c k1) 5 times, c T T T) 6 times, k1 T TB *** k1 (centre st.), repeat *** — *** (227)

Knit one row. Decrease row. Purl one row. Decrease row. Knit one row.

**COLOUR CHANGE L14**

8th pattern row : *** T T T k1 (c k1) 5 times, c T T T (k1 T T T (c k1) 5 times, c T T T) 4 times, k1 T T T (c k1) 5 times, c k1 T T TB *** , k1 (centre st.), repeat *** — *** (219)

Knit one row. Decrease row. Purl one row. **COLOUR CHANGE L1**

Decrease row. Knit one row.

9th pattern row : *** T T k1 (c k1) 5 times, c T T T (k1 T T T (c k1) 5 times, c T T T) 4 times, k1 T T T (c k1) 5 times, c k1 T TB *** , k1 (centre st.), repeat *** — *** (215)

Knit one row. **COLOUR CHANGE L16**

Decrease row. Purl one row. Decrease row. Knit one row.

10th pattern row : *** T T (c k1) 5 times, c T T T (k1 T T T (c k1) 5 times, c T T T) 4 times, k1 T T T (c k1) 5 times, c T TB *** , k1 (centre st.), repeat *** — *** (211)

Knit one row. **COLOUR CHANGE L15**

Decrease row. Purl one row. Decrease row. Knit one row.

11th pattern row : *** T T (c k1) 4 times, c T T T (k1 T T T (c k1) 5 times, c T T T) 4 times, k1 T T T (c k1) 4 times, c T TB *** , k1 (centre st.), repeat *** — *** (203)

Knit one row. **COLOUR CHANGE L14**

Decrease row. Purl one row. Decrease row. Knit one row.

**COLOUR CHANGE L1**

12th pattern row : *** T k1 (c k1) 3 times, c T T T (k1 T T T (c k1) 5 times, c T T T) 4 times, k1 T T T (c k1) 3 times, c k1 TB *** , k1 (centre st.), repeat *** — *** (195)

Knit one row. Decrease row. Purl one row. **COLOUR CHANGE L16**

Decrease row. Knit one row.

13th pattern row : *** T (c k1) twice, c T T T (k1 T T T (c k1) 5 times, c T T T) 4 times, k1 T T T (c k1) twice, c TB *** , k1 (centre st.), repeat *** — *** (183)

Knit one row. Decrease row. Purl one row. **COLOUR CHANGE L15**

Decrease row. Knit one row.

14th pattern row : *** T k1 T T (k1 T T T (c k1) 5 times, c T T T) 4 times, k1 T T k1 TB *** k1 (centre st.), repeat *** — *** (163)

Knit one row. Decrease row. Purl one row. **COLOUR CHANGE L14**

Decrease row. Knit one row.

15th pattern row : *** T (k1 T T T (c k1) 5 times, c T T T) 4 times, k1 TB *** k1 (centre st.), repeat *** — *** (151)

Knit one row. **COLOUR CHANGE L1**

Decrease row. Purl one row. Decrease row. Knit one row.

**COLOUR CHANGE L15**

16th pattern row : *** T T T (c k1) 5 times, c T T T (k1 T T T (c k1) 5 times, c T T T) twice,
k1 T T T (c k1) 5 times, c T T TB *** , k1 (centre st.), repeat *** — *** (143)

Knit one row. Decrease row. Purl one row. Decrease row. Knit one row.

**COLOUR CHANGE L14**

17th pattern row : *** T T T (c k1) 3 times, c T T T (k1 T T T (c k1) 5 times, c T T T) twice,
k1 T T T (c k1) 3 times, c T T TB *** , k1 (centre st.), repeat *** — *** (127)

Knit one row. Decrease row. Purl one row. **COLOUR CHANGE L1**

Decrease row. Knit one row.

18th pattern row : *** T T c k1 c T T T (k1 T T T (c k1) 5 times, c T T T) twice,
k1 T T T c k1 c T TB *** , k1 (centre st.), repeat *** — *** (107)

Knit one row. **COLOUR CHANGE L15**

Decrease row. Purl one row. Decrease row. Knit one row.

19th pattern row : *** T T T (k1 T T T (c k1) 5 times, c T T T) twice, k1 T T TB ***
k1 (centre st.), repeat *** — *** (87)

Knit one row. **COLOUR CHANGE L14**

Decrease row. Purl one row. Decrease row. Knit one row.

**COLOUR CHANGE L1**

20th pattern row : *** T T T T (c k1) 5 times, c T T T, k1 T T T (c k1) 5 times, c T T T TB ***
k1 (centre st.), repeat *** — *** (75)

Knit one row. Decrease row. Purl one row. **COLOUR CHANGE L15**

Decrease row. Knit one row.

21st pattern row : *** T T T (c k1) 4 times, c T T T, k1 T T T (c k1) 4 times, c T T TB ***
k1 (centre st.), repeat *** — *** (63)

Knit one row. **COLOUR CHANGE L14**

Decrease row. Purl one row. Decrease row. Knit one row.

**COLOUR CHANGE L1**

*The Belinda Shoulder Shawl*

22nd pattern row : *** T T (c k1) 3 times, c T T T, k1 T T T (c k1) 3 times, c T TB *** k1 (centre st.), repeat *** — *** (51)

Knit one row. Decrease row. Purl one row. **COLOUR CHANGE L14**

Decrease row. Knit one row.

23rd pattern row : *** T k1 c k1 c T T T, k1 T T T c k1 c k1 TB *** k1 (centre st.), repeat *** — *** (35)

Knit one row. **COLOUR CHANGE L1**

Decrease row. Purl one row. Decrease row. Knit one row.

**COLOUR CHANGE L14**

24th pattern row : 3T c 3T c T c T c 3TB, k1 (centre st.), 3T c T c T c 3T c 3TB (19)

Knit one row. Decrease row. Purl one row. **COLOUR CHANGE L1**

Decrease row.

Leave the remaining 11 sts. on a spare needle.

With right side of work facing, and using **SHADE L1,** pick up and knit 73 sts. along the RIGHT-HAND side, **CASTING UP AFTER EACH STITCH, (i.e. K1 c K1 c K1 c.....finishing with c);** then knit across the 11 sts. from the spare needle, then pick up and knit 73 sts. from the LEFT-HAND side, **CASTING UP BEFORE EACH STITCH, (i.e. c K1 c K1 c K1.....finishing with K1).** **(Total 303 sts.)**

Knit one complete row, taking up the first 'pin' stitch from the RIGHT-HAND side with the last stitch.

Next row — K1 (T c) 67 times, (3T c) 5 times, 3T (centre), (c 3T) 5 times, (c T) 67 times, k1 taking up the first pin stitch from the LEFT-HAND side with the last stitch. (291)

**NOTE** : From now on the 'pin' stitches will be worked, one by one, with the last stitch of each row.

Knit one row. **COLOUR CHANGE L14**

Knit one row. Purl one row. Knit one row. Knit one row.

**COLOUR CHANGE L15**

Pattern row — K1 (k1 T T T (c k1) 5 times, c T T T) 8 times,
k1 (centre st.), (T T T (c k1) 5 times, c T T T k1) 8 times, k1 (291)

Knit one row. Knit one row. Purl one row. Knit one row. Knit one row.

**COLOUR CHANGE L16**

Pattern row — K1 (k1 T T T (c k1) 5 times, c T T T) 8 times,
k1 (centre st.), (T T T (c k1) 5 times, c T T T k1) 8 times, k1 (291)

Knit one row. Knit one row. Purl one row. Knit one row. Knit one row.

**COLOUR CHANGE L18**

Pattern row — K1 (k1 T T T (c k1) 5 times, c T T T) 8 times,
k1 (centre st.), (T T T (c k1) 5 times, c T T T k1) 8 times, k1 (291)

Knit one row. Knit one row, taking up the last of the 22 'pin' stitches.

Next row — Knit and continue, knitting up the 10 sts. from the cast-off straight side of the border scallops.

Knit one complete row and continue, knitting up the 10 sts. from the cast-on straight side of the border scallops.

Purl one complete row. (311 sts.)

**CAST OFF LOOSELY.**

**DARN IN ENDS, AND CUT OFF AFTER DRESSING**

**TO DRESS SHAWL :** Wash **BY HAND ONLY** in lukewarm soapy water, squeezing gently. Rinse in lukewarm water. Roll up in a towel to absorb excess moisture. Stretch out to dry to shape, away from heat or sun, and pin out scallops at points on to a white sheet, and dry flat.

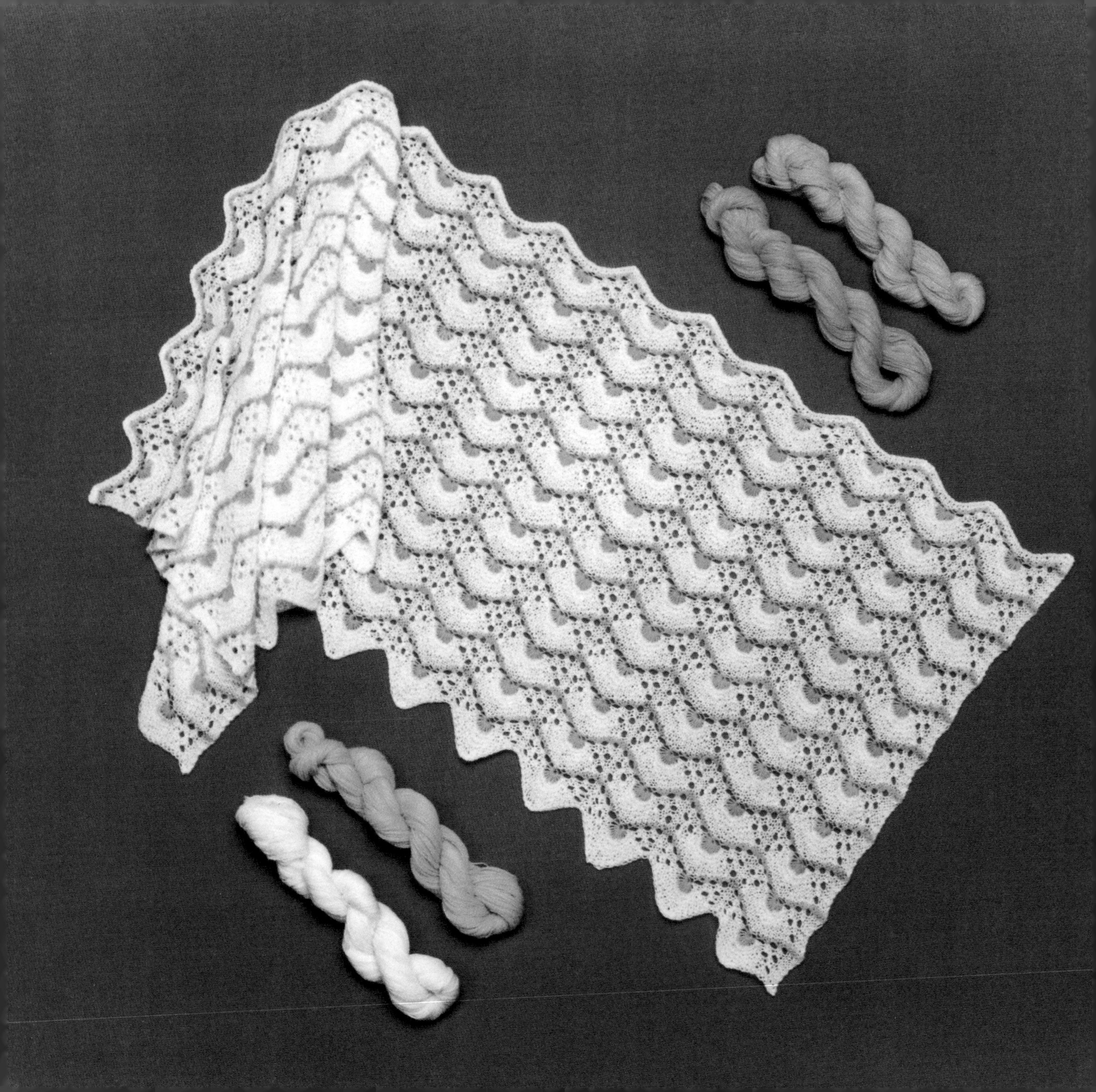

# *Cockleshell Stole*

## KNITTED IN 2-PLY LACE WOOL

**Size — 64'' x 20'' (160cm x 50cm)**

**MATERIALS** : 3 hanks — 2-ply lace wool — main colour
1 hank — 2-ply lace wool — contrast colour (CC)
1 circular needle — size 9 (3.75mm) — 24" (60cm) long

The Cockleshell scarf has been a very popular item for many years. This stole is designed to be knitted the opposite way to the traditional scarf — the 'shells' being worked along the length of the stole rather than across the width.

It is knitted here with contrast colours included, but can also be knitted in a single colour.

**EDGING** :
An edging of 3 garter stitches is maintained at both ends of every row throughout the stole. These 3 plus 3 stitches are **NOT** included in the 12 row pattern detail.

**SPECIAL ABBREVIATION** :
**"K twice"** — Knit into the front **AND** back of the next stitch
Where "K twice" is used, the stitch referred to is the "c" (cast up) from the previous row.
Example : Row 2 — starts with 19 sts. — work, K1, K twice, k15, K twice, k1 — increased to 21 sts.

**CONTRAST COLOUR** :
**"CC"** marked alongside rows 9 and 10, of the pattern, indicates that these rows are worked in a contrast colour. Only a small quantity of the contrast colour is required and the knitter may of course use a selection of differing contrast colours if so desired.

# *Cockleshell Stole*

## COCKLESHELL STITCH PATTERN

| | ROW | | |
|---|---|---|---|
| | 1 | K1, cT, k13, Tc, k1 | (19) |
| | 2 | K1, K twice, k15, K twice, k1 | (21) |
| | 3 | Knit | |
| | 4 | Knit | |
| | 5 | K1, cT cT, k11, Tc Tc, k1 | (21) |
| | 6 | K1, K twice k1 K twice, k13, K twice k1 K twice, k1 | (25) |
| | 7 | Knit | |
| | 8 | Knit | |
| **CC** | 9 | K1, cT cT cT, (c k1) 11 times, c, Tc Tc Tc, k1 | (37) |
| **CC** | 10 | (K1, K twice) 3 times, slip next and every alternate stitch on to RIGHT-HAND needle (13 sts.), at the same time dropping the 12 'c' stitches from the last row. Knit together the 13 sts. which were slipped, (K twice, k1) 3 times | (19) |
| | 11 | Knit | |
| | 12 | Knit | |

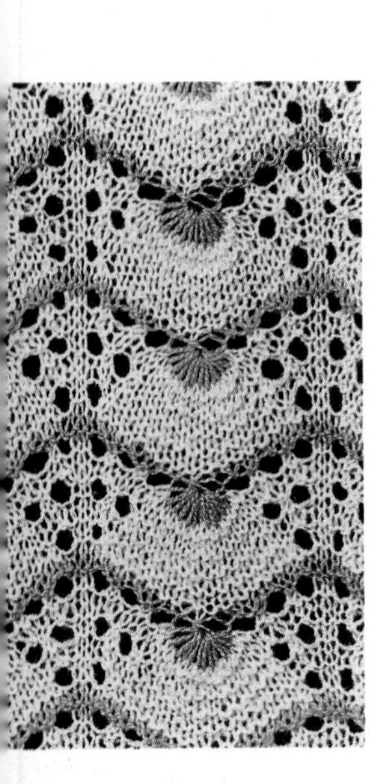

## WORKING INSTRUCTIONS

With No.9 needle and using main colour, cast on 348 stitches **VERY** loosely (2 needle method).
Knit 3 rows.
Start pattern sequence — K3, (pattern) 18 times, k3
Work complete 12 row pattern sequence 11 times in all.
Knit one further row.

## CAST OFF LOOSELY

**TO DRESS STOLE :** Wash **BY HAND ONLY** in lukewarm soapy water, squeezing gently. Rinse in lukewarm water. Roll up in a towel to absorb excess moisture. Dry flat on a white sheet, away from heat or sun, pinning out to size and shape, ensuring that each shell is shaped.

## ACKNOWLEDGMENTS

I would like to thank everyone who has helped in any way with the production of this book — the staff of The Shetland Times, my friends at Jamieson & Smith, my models — Clare and baby Kara, Smiths of Lerwick for lending dresses for photographs, Islesburgh Community Centre for facilities provided and John who photographed my work.

A few years ago "the persuaders" — Margaret Sandison formerly of The Shetland Times Bookshop and Eva Smith of Jamieson & Smith — first suggested I should put some of my work into a book. My thanks to them for encouraging me — I hope they are not disappointed with my efforts!

My husband and family have given me more support than I can record — they have been very patient with me and helped in many ways. To them, my very special thanks. Without their constant support and encouragement this book could not have been produced.

# NOTES